# Following the Way of Jesus

VOLUME 6
in the
**Church's**
**Teachings**
**for a**
**Changing**
**World**
series

BY MICHAEL B. CURRY

With reflections by
Megan Castellan, Kellan Day, Nora Gallagher,
Broderick Greer, Anthony Guillén, and Robert Wright

Church Publishing
NEW YORK

Church Publishing
19 East 34th Street
New York, NY 10016
www.churchpublishing.org

Cover art: *A lo lejos*, © Revd Ernesto Lozada-Uzuriaga Steele
Cover design by Jennifer Kopec, 2Pug Design
Typeset by Beth Oberholtzer

**Library of Congress Cataloging-in-Publication Data**
A record of this book is available from the Library of Congress.

ISBN-13: 978-0-89869-969-2 (pbk.)
ISBN-13: 978-0-89869-970-8 (ebook)

*Printed in the United States of America*

# Contents

# Introduction

Jesus did not establish an institution, though institutions can serve his cause. He did not organize a political party, though his teachings have a profound impact on politics. Jesus did not even found a religion. No, Jesus began a movement, fueled by his Spirit, a movement whose purpose was and is to change the face of the earth from the nightmare it often is into the dream that God intends.

A few months ago I was being interviewed about this Jesus Movement for a conversation in one of our dioceses. The interviewer pointedly asked me, "The church has a way of jumping on the trendiest bandwagon, then when a new one comes along, jumping ship and getting on the new one. It's sort of the Flavor of the Month syndrome. So is the Jesus Movement the newest trend, the newest Flavor of the Month?"

It's a great question because behind it is the question of what is really at stake. And I believe the faithfulness and effectiveness of the Church—the whole purpose of our ministry and existence—is at stake. We are, after all, first and foremost, the Episcopal branch of the Jesus Movement.

That's why I think it's so important that anyone thinking about the practice of Episcopal ministry for the coming century seriously consider the question: what is this Jesus Movement, and what does it have to do with ministry in the Episcopal Church? It's why I took time to develop sermons I've preached since I became presiding bishop into a set of opening chapters, and it's why I'm so grateful to the leaders who have joined me by sharing their reflections on ministry priorities for the Jesus Movement:

- Lots of people love Megan Castellan's blogging at https://redshoesfunnyshirt.com. In her chapter, she focuses on evangelism and spreading the Good News we've received from Jesus—Good News that will surely change a world. Megan is the Assistant Rector at St. Paul's Episcopal Church in Kansas City, Missouri, and Northern Youth Network coordinator for the Diocese of West Missouri.

- Anthony Guillén, Director of Ethnic Ministries for the Episcopal Church, brings many perspectives and voices together in his reflection on launching new ministries in multicultural contexts.

- Kellan Day offers key insights on young adult ministry, an area that is crucial if we are going to proclaim the gospel for generations to come. She serves as the Young Adult Missioner in the Diocese of Western Michigan.

- Broderick Greer is a priest on staff at Grace-St. Luke's Episcopal Church in Memphis, Tennessee. His videos and writings at www.broderickgreer.com include equal measures challenge and inspiration, and he writes the chapter on the practice of racial reconciliation and justice.

- One of my favorite authors (who happens to be an Episcopalian), Nora Gallagher shares her thoughts on ministry that embraces the kingdom of God right here on the earth. Her books include *Practicing Resurrection* and *Things Seen and Unseen*.

- And Robert Wright, the bishop of the Diocese of Atlanta, introduces us to the whole concept of adaptive change, or how to turn institutions and people in new directions and truly lead a movement.

This volume is part of the Church's Teachings for a Changing World series, a collection of books that reintroduce the essentials of Episcopal teaching and faith. Edited by my friends and colleagues Stephanie Spellers and Eric Law, each of these books tries to bring a combination of deep content and true accessibility. We want anyone to feel comfortable opening these pages: church leaders facing major challenges in their local community, seminarians studying for ordination exams, newcomers who've heard about this "Jesus Movement" and want to know how it affects the way Episcopalians practice our faith. Most of all, I pray that what we lay down here will lift up readers of all kinds, and send you out fully energized to follow in the loving, liberating, and life-giving way of Jesus Christ.

# Chapter 1

# Welcome to the Jesus Movement

So when [the disciples] had come together, they asked [Jesus], "Lord, is this the time when you will restore the kingdom to Israel?" He replied, "It is not for you to know the times or periods that the Father has set by his own authority. But you will receive power when the Holy Spirit has come upon you; and you will be my witnesses in Jerusalem, in all Judea and Samaria, and to the ends of the earth."

(Acts 1:6–8)

Ultimately, the Jesus Movement is a metaphor. Images, metaphors, and forms of symbolic speech are a way of helping you to get at more deep and complex things in accessible and memorable ways. This Jesus Movement isn't a twenty-first-century invention or a throwback to 1960s "Jesus Freaks" or a rhetorical concoction of my making. We're talking about going forward as a church by going back to our deepest roots as disciples of Jesus Christ.

New Testament scholars and others who look at early Christian origins often refer to the Christian movement in its beginnings

**The Jesus Movement:** We're following Jesus into loving, liberating, life-giving relationship with God, with each other, and with creation.

as the "Jesus Movement." Rodney Stark, a sociologist of religion who has studied early Christian origins and the expansion and growth of Christianity, has written the suggestively titled book *The Triumph of Christianity: How the Jesus Movement Became the World's Largest Religion.* It's not an adaptation of Christian triumphalism but a description of the evolution of the movement Jesus inaugurated into the Church.

Stark is specific and prolific on this topic. He explains the way Christianity grew as a movement to bring new life to Judaism and to broken people:

> Christianity served as a revitalization movement that arose in response to the misery, chaos, fear and brutality of life in the urban Greco-Roman world. . . . To cities filled with the homeless and impoverished, Christianity offered charity as well as hope. To cities filled with newcomers and strangers, Christianity offered an immediate basis for attachments. To cities filled with orphans and widows, Christianity provided a new and expanded sense of family. To cities torn by violent ethnic strife, Christianity offered a new basis for social solidarity.[1]

So when we use the phrase the "Jesus Movement," we're actually pointing back to the earliest days of Jesus's teaching and his followers moving in his revolutionary footsteps in the power of the Spirit. Together with them, we're following Jesus and growing loving, liberating, life-giving relationship with God, with each other, and with creation.

The late Verna Dozier shares this understanding. A brilliant black lay theologian and educator, her last published book was

---

1. Rodney Stark, *The Triumph of Christianity: How the Jesus Movement Became the World's Largest Religion* (New York: HarperCollins, 2011), 161.

titled, *The Dream of God: A Call to Return*[2]. She would have rec-
ognized the Jesus Movement as a call to return to our deepest origins as Christians, to return to the roots of our very life, as people
of the Way, as disciples of the Lord Jesus. It's a call to return so
that we can truly march forward, following the way of Jesus.

## God on the Move

There's no denying it: Jesus began a movement. That's why his
invitations to folk who joined him are filled with so many active
verbs. In John 1:39 Jesus calls disciples with the words, "Come
and see." In Matthew, Mark, and Luke, he asks others to "Follow
me." And at the end of the Gospels, he sent his first disciples out
with the word, "Go . . ." As in, "Go therefore and make disciples
of all nations" (Matt. 28:19). As in, "Go into all the world and
proclaim the good news to the whole creation" (Mark 16:15).

In Acts 1 he uses even more movement language: "But you will
receive power when the Holy Spirit has come upon you; and you
will be my witnesses in Jerusalem, in all Judea and Samaria, and
to the ends of the earth" (v. 8). If you look at the Bible, listen to
it, and watch how the Spirit of God unfolds in the sacred story, I
think you'll notice a pattern. You cannot help but notice that there
really is a movement of God in the world.

If you don't believe me, ask Abraham and Sarah. They were
ready to enjoy their pension and their senior years. Then God
called and said: "Go from your country and your kindred and your
father's house to the land that I will show you. I will make of you
a great nation" (Gen. 12:1–2).

Beyond their own desires Abraham and Sarah found themselves a part of the movement of God. On their journey they joined
up with a woman named Hagar, and Abraham, Sarah, and Hagar

---

2. Verna Dozier, *The Dream of God: A Call to Return* (New York: Church
Publishing, 2006).

were a family. (It was a dysfunctional family, but a family none-theless.) Abraham, Sarah, and Hagar are the ancestors of Judaism, Christianity, and Islam. They're proof that God has a movement.

If you still don't believe me, ask Moses. According to the biblical book of Exodus, Moses was born of Hebrew slaves in Egypt. But due to mysterious circumstances, Moses was adopted by a loving Egyptian princess and nursed by his Hebrew mother. In his adulthood this dual nature caused him quite an identity crisis. He had to wonder: "Am I a slave or a slave master?"

In the midst of this crisis he was forced to flee Egypt. He eventually married a woman named Zipporah whose father Jethro was a well-off businessman. Moses ran the business and everything was cozy, until he ran into a burning bush. Of course it was God. Instead of asking Moses to enjoy the comfortable life, God challenged him to join the movement, to leave the comfort of Jethro's business and go back to Egypt, back to the land of his people, back to the Hebrew slaves and Egyptian slave owners. But now he would return as liberator to set the captives free, just like the old spiritual says . . .

> When Israel was in Egypt's land (Let my people go)
> Oppressed so hard they could not stand (Let my people go)
>
> Go down, Moses
> Way down in Egypt land
> And tell old Pharaoh
> Let my people go.

And Moses went, because he was part of God's movement.

You could ask Isaiah, who was in the temple when he heard the call from God. Isaiah was comfortable—he rather liked living in the capital city of Jerusalem, and residing in the temple, where there was always good, well-executed "high church" liturgy. But God called, "Who will go for us?" and Isaiah said, "Here I am; send me" (Isa. 6:8).

You could ask Queen Esther, challenged by Mordecai to risk her regal privileges and go to the king to save her people. "Who knows?" Mordecai asked her. "Perhaps you have come to royal dignity for just such a time as this." Her response: "I will go to the king . . . and if I perish, I perish" (Esther 4:14–16).

Ask any of the disciples who left their nets to follow Jesus. They heard the Jesus who said, "Go into all the world and proclaim the good news to the whole creation" (Mark 16:15). They heard his call to "[g]o therefore and make disciples of all nations, baptizing them in the name of the Father and of the Son and of the Holy Spirit, and teaching them to obey everything that I have commanded you." And they heard his reassurance that "I am with you always, to the end of the age" (Matt. 28:20). And so they went. And so do we.

## The Shape of the Jesus Movement

In the mid-1990s biblical scholar Elisabeth Schüssler Fiorenza studied the earliest days of Christianity, a period she called the "Jesus Movement." In her study of the New Testament, she noticed several things that matter as we consider the topic of ministry for the movement.

First, the movement was Christ-centered—completely focused on Jesus and his way. In fact, if you look at the Acts of the Apostles in the New Testament, long before Christianity was ever called the Church, or even Christianity, it was called "the Way." The way of Jesus was the way. The Spirit of Jesus, the Spirit of God, that sweet, sweet Spirit, infused their spirits and took over.

William Temple, one of the great archbishops of Canterbury from the last century, once said that there is no use just telling him to be like Jesus. He couldn't do it . . . except with the Spirit of Christ.

According to biblical scholar Elizabeth Schüssler Fiorenza, the Jesus Movement 1) centered on Jesus, 2) eliminated poverty and hunger, and 3) integrated people at all levels of society.

> It's no good giving me a play like Hamlet or King Lear and telling me to write a play like that. Shakespeare could do it. I can't. And it is no good showing me a life like the life of Jesus and telling me to live a life like that. Jesus could do it; I can't. But if the genius of Shakespeare could come and live in me, then I could write plays like his. And if the Spirit of Jesus could come and live in me, then I could live a life like his.[3]

When the Spirit that lived so fully in Jesus inhabits us, then we have a chance to live like him. That's precisely what happened to the early followers of his way. They began to look like Jesus. Folk in Antioch saw them and nicknamed them "little Christs."

The second mark of the movement is this: following the way of Jesus, they abolished poverty and hunger in their community. Some might say they made poverty history. The Acts of the Apostles calls this abolition of poverty one of the "signs and wonders" which became an invitation to others to follow Jesus too, and change the world.

> Now the whole group of those who believed were of one heart and soul, and no one claimed private ownership of any possessions, but everything they owned was held in common. With great power the apostles gave their testimony to the resurrection of the Lord Jesus, and great grace was upon them all. There was not a needy person among them, for as many as owned lands or houses sold them and brought the proceeds of what was sold. (Acts 4:32–34)

It didn't take a miracle. The Bible says they simply shared everything they had. The movement moved them in that peculiar way.

Third, they learned how to become more than a collection of individual self-interests. They found themselves becoming a countercultural community, one where Jews and Gentiles, circumcised

---

3. William Temple, quoted in John Stott's *Radical Disciple: Some Neglected Aspects of Our Calling* (Downers Grove, IL: Intervarsity Press, 2010), 37.

and uncircumcised, had equal standing, and even slave girls could speak and prophesy, full of the Spirit (Acts 15:1–21; 16:16).

I was a child and I remember my father taking me to meetings of the Union of Black Episcopalians, which was organized to eradicate racism from the Episcopal Church. At that time, it was known as the Union of Black Clergy and Laity.

I remember some of those giants, now of blessed memory: Mattie Hopkins, Austin Cooper, Quinton Primo, John Burgess, Fred Williams, Jimmy Woodruff. The Union was founded to eradicate racism, but we understood that was not the ultimate goal. That was one step toward the goal. The ultimate goal has always been bigger than that.

At the end of the Montgomery bus boycott in 1956, someone asked Martin Luther King Jr. what the end or goal of the boycott really was. And he answered—you can almost hear him thinking out loud—"The end is the end of segregation." But wait—it's more than that: "The end is reconciliation." No, he finally concluded, the real end "is the creation of the beloved community."[4]

That's when they were clearly part of the Jesus Movement, because they were turning the world upside down, just like he did, just like his followers have from the start. And they weren't doing it for their own gain, but to join Jesus in creating a community where everybody is beloved, no one is hungry, no one is left out, all are equally children of God.

## Partners in the God Movement

We need baptized people who are committed to living and witnessing to the way of Jesus. I still remember the day that became crystal clear for me.

---

4. Martin Luther King Jr., "Speech at Conclusion of Montgomery Bus Boycott," 1956, http://www.thekingcenter.org/king-philosophy.

It was morning. I was in court with someone from my congregation when everything stopped. The judged stopped the proceedings and announced that two planes had just crashed into the World Trade Center.

Everything really did just stop. I was scheduled for a Eucharist with baptism and confirmations that night. Suddenly we were faced with a very real question: Should we go on with the service? Or maybe have a memorial service instead and do baptisms and confirmations later?

We talked, we prayed, and we realized—no, this is precisely when the church must be the church. So we included prayers for those who died, for those who suffered, for our enemies, for ourselves, and for the world. And we did baptize new followers of Jesus. We confirmed disciples of Jesus who were reaffirming and reorienting themselves to follow the way of Jesus.

In one of those moments when all of the distractions and props were stripped away, we were called back to the essence of who we are and what we are here for as the church, the body of Christ, the Jesus Movement in the world. I am more convinced of that necessity every day. We need people who will proclaim by word and example the Good News of God in Christ, who will love justice, live mercy, and walk humbly with God, just like Jesus.

Pastor and biblical scholar Clarence Jordan was one of those people. In 1942, he worked with a team to found Koinonia Farm in Georgia, welcoming people of different races to live and work together, caring for each other and for the land. They called it a "demonstration plot" for the God Movement.

His word choice wasn't accidental. In the 1960s, he wrote a Southern-folk, liberation-minded version of the New Testament called the Cotton Patch Gospel. When he translated the Greek New Testament and came to the word *basileia*, usually read as "kingdom," he decided it was more like a movement or "something that gets underway spontaneously."[5] He spoke of it as the God Movement.

Jordan was one the earliest white leaders to take up the civil rights cause, but even then his ultimate goal was clear. "There must be a greater and deeper movement than the Civil Rights Movement." Jordan kept his eye on "the God Movement, the stirring of His mighty Spirit of love, peace, humility, forgiveness, joy and reconciliation in the hearts of all of us."[6]

Jordan once offered wise counsel to a young peace worker named Craig Peters. It is worth repeating today:

> I am increasingly convinced that Jesus thought of his messages as not dead-ending in a static institution but as a mighty flow of spirit which would penetrate every nook and cranny of man's personal and social life. . . . I really don't think we can ever renew the church until we stop thinking of it as an institution and start thinking of it as a movement.[7]

He was right. Ministry in this moment—Episcopal ministry or ministry in any denomination or tradition—has to serve more than an institution. It has to serve the movement.

---

5. Charles Marsh, *The Beloved Community: How Faith Shapes Social Justice, from the Civil Rights Movement to Today* (New York: Basic Books, 2005), 81.

6. Marsh, 81.

7. Marsh, 81.

## QUESTIONS FOR THE ROAD . . .

1. The Jesus Movement is defined this way: "We're following Jesus into loving, liberating, life-giving relationship with God, with each other, and with creation." What do you think and feel about this definition? What parts resonate and what parts make you curious?

2. Curry and others see Christianity as primarily a movement, one that expresses itself in an institution but should always be on the move. What are the benefits of this way of understanding the church? What are the limitations?

3. Have you ever seen a Christian who was clearly participating in the Jesus Movement? What was this person doing and saying? How did others respond?

# Chapter 2

# Centered in the Way of Love

There is a moment in every celebration of the Holy Eucharist when we bear witness to being the Jesus Movement: the reading of the Holy Gospel. In that moment Jesus Christ clearly is at the center, and everything revolves around him and the Gospel.

What happens? We have been sitting to listen to other parts of Holy Scripture. But when we read the Gospel, we stand up. Very often there is a procession to the middle of the congregation. Christ at the center.

The procession is often adorned with acolytes bearing candles, maybe a crucifer bearing the cross. There is music: sometimes a hymn, sometimes a fanfare. Deacons—the people called in the Jesus Movement to stand as a bridge between the church and the world—read the Gospel. The bishop, if he or she has been wearing a mitre, takes it off and might even hold the bishop's staff. The Gospel book may be kissed and censed with a thurible full of incense. Everyone wherever they are in the room turns and faces the place where the Gospel is read.

We're watching as the entire room reorients itself around the Gospel, the Way of Jesus. Christ at the center.

That's the Jesus Movement. We are a community of people whose lives are constantly being reoriented around Jesus, bearing

Jesus came to change us, to turn us toward himself, so we could live like the God who, according to 1 John 4:8, is Love.

witness to his way, not the world's way. We are living his way of love, not our own.

## The Greatest Commandment

Athanasius, one of our fourth century church ancestors, once said, "God became human in order that humans might become like God."[8] In other words, Jesus came to change us, to turn us toward himself. He didn't necessarily come to give us omnipotent power like God, but so we could live like the God who, according to 1 John 4:8, is Love.

Jesus places that love at the center in Matthew 22. The Pharisees heard that Jesus had silenced the Sadducees. So they got together, and one of them, a lawyer, asked a question designed to test Jesus. "Teacher, which commandment in the law is the greatest?" Jesus said to him, "'You shall love the Lord your God with all your heart, and with all your soul, and with all your mind.' This is the greatest and first commandment. And a second is like it: 'You shall love your neighbor as yourself.' On these two commandments hang all the law and the prophets" (Matt. 22:36–40).

If you look in the New Testament, you'll notice that Jesus had a number of conversations with lawyers, often engaging in a contest of questions and ideas. Those lawyers pushed Jesus to make some of his most important statements. This particular lawyer was asking Jesus to spell it out: What is the core? What is the essence? What is God really getting at? What was the Supreme Court ruling by which the truth of all religious law and prophecy could be measured?

Jesus answered by drawing on two teachings of Moses. The first part—you shall love the Lord your God with all your heart, all your soul—deals with our relationship with Jesus Christ and the God who created us (think of it as evangelism, the practice of helping other people to find their own loving relationship with God and their place in the Beloved Community). The second

---

8. Athanasius, *On the Incarnation*, 54:3.

part—you shall love your neighbor as yourself—outlines our relationship with each other as children of the God who created us (that's reconciliation, loving and seeking the face of God in that person close to you and the one far, far away). And it's not a stretch to call the earth our neighbor, our mother—God wants this love to embrace her as well (that's creation care, every effort we make to embrace and honor presence of God revealed in the glory of creation).

Jesus couldn't have been more clear. Religion is completely and totally about the love of God and love of neighbor. The core of the way of Jesus is love. If it's not about love, it's not about God.

## What Kind of Love Is This?

As usual, Jesus doesn't just answer the lawyer's question. He shows him. Notice that Jesus has this conversation with the lawyer during Holy Week. That's not insignificant. Jesus is on his way to the cross. Jesus didn't go to that cross for himself. He did not do it for his own sins, for anything he could get out of it, but for us, for the world, for the human family. It was a purely selfless act that demonstrated for us the path to salvation and reconciliation with God and each other.

Now it's easy to get schmaltzy and turn love into sentimentality, but don't be deceived. The love of God is shocking and sacrificial. It is not self-centered but other-directed. It seeks the good and the welfare of the other before self-interest.

Something in every one of us knows this is fundamentally true, and we want it for ourselves. It's probably why couples love 1 Corinthians 13 so much. In all the years I was a parish priest doing weddings, when they were choosing Scriptures for the service, nine times out of ten they picked this one for the second lesson: "If I speak in the tongues of mortals and of angels, but do not have love, I am a noisy gong or a clanging cymbal. . . . And now faith, hope, and love abide, these three; and the greatest of these is love" (1 Cor. 13:1, 13).

The truth is that Paul wasn't thinking about weddings or marriage when he wrote these words to the church at Corinth. He was dealing with a church fight. Folk had divided into factions. The rich were segregating from the poor at Holy Communion. Somebody else was getting drunk at the table. Somebody was sleeping with somebody else's wife. Somebody was suing somebody else in the church. And they were all arguing over who was going to heaven. How did Paul know? The church gossip told him so.

This was one messed up church, like all the members were characters on ABC's *Scandal*. Everybody was out for Number 1. Their selfishness and self-centeredness were destroying the church, and love was the only cure. That's when Paul told them love is not jealous, rude, or boastful. Love does not insist on its own way. Love seeks the common good, not just what's in it for me. Love looks for what is just and fair—it doesn't just look out for Number 1. And we need it—in marriages, in churches, in the Episcopal Church and the Anglican Communion, in the halls of Congress, the Supreme Court, and the United Nations.

If you had asked me a few months ago what is the opposite of love, I probably would have answered hate. And there's truth in that. But that's really not the answer. The opposite of love is not hate. The opposite of love is selfishness. And it is this unenlightened self-centeredness that gives rise to hatred, bigotry, and violence—or, to say it in the way of Christian tradition, sin.

On the cross, we say Jesus conquered and freed us from sin. That's because the way of the cross is the way of unselfish, sacrificial love. "As the Father has loved me, so have I loved you; abide in my love. . . . No one has greater love than this, to lay down one's life for one's friends" (John 15:9, 13). This way is the opposite of hate, the only way to defeat sin.

The people who have changed the world for the good have consistently been people whose lives have been characterized by this

"As the Father has loved me, so have I loved you; abide in my love. . . . No one has greater love than this, to lay down one's life for one's friends" (John 15:9, 13).

kind of non-self-centered, other-directed, sacrificial love. Go to the Nobel Peace Prize website and read the biographies of the awardees: Mahatma Gandhi in India; Lech Walesa in Poland; Nelson Mandela in South Africa; Malala of Pakistan, fighting for girls' rights to education. It's like a spiritual exercise, studying their witness.

But this love is not just present in Nobel Prize recipients. Think about the people who have changed your life for the good. They have loved you, even when it cost them or pained them, until you became more than you would have been otherwise. They taught you the way of love.

## Turn the World Upside Down

Nobody understood the power of Jesus's way of love better than the disciples whose lives he turned upside down. As Jesus passed along the Sea of Galilee, he saw Simon and his brother Andrew casting a net into the sea. And Jesus said to them, "Follow me and I will make you fish for people." And immediately they left their nets and followed him (Mark 1:16–17).

Think about the first disciples who followed the way of Jesus: Simon Peter and Andrew, James and John. Do you remember what they did for a living? They were fishermen. Now we aren't talking about recreational trout fishing. These men fished for a living. But think for a moment. I have yet to see one instance in the whole New Testament when these professional fishermen ever caught any fish without Jesus telling them how to do it . . . and Jesus was a carpenter!

This is not the A-Team of apostolic discipleship we're talking about here. I think the Bible is trying to tell us something.

In chapter 10 of the Gospel of Mark, James and John, the Zebedee brothers, come up to Jesus when the other disciples aren't around to ask him for good jobs in the kingdom. Jesus had been waxing eloquent about the coming of God's reign, and these two thought they might get jobs in his new government.

We all know how this system works. When Republicans win, Republicans get jobs. When Democrats win, Democrats get the jobs. They figured when their man won, they could get good jobs. The other disciples hit the roof when they found out. And I would dare say Jesus wanted to pull his hair out.

But that's not all of it. Matthew's Gospel tells the same story, and in his version James and John send their mother to ask Jesus for these special favors. They send their mother to do their dirty work. Again, I remind you, this is not the A-Team of apostolic discipleship we're talking about here.

Or let's go to the Last Supper and Good Friday. Peter promised him, "Lord, don't worry about a thing, I've got your back." Then Peter does everything he can to leave Jesus in the dust. If there's a Simon Peter who says he's got your back, you better run backwards.

We need to thank God that Jesus had the spiritual foresight to break with the custom and tradition of his day and called women disciples. Only the sisters were there at the cross with the one brother. If it hadn't been for Mary Magdalene and the women disciples, we might not know to this day that Jesus rose from the dead.

When the going got tough, the apostles got going. With the exception of one male disciple and the women disciples, they all failed him. Betrayed him. Abandoned him. Denied him. No, these men are not the A-Team of apostolic discipleship.

Hold onto all that and *then* read the rest of the story. This sorry bunch kept following Jesus, long after it seemed he was gone. And the book of Acts tells the story of how the Spirit of Jesus took hold of them, and the Way of Jesus became their way. This same group of timid, frail, fragile, sinful, mortal, normal, and ever-so-fallible human beings were described by people who experienced their later ministry as leaders who were turning the world upside down. Tradition has it that they spread out and evangelized the known world. Each one of them except for John the Beloved was probably executed as a martyr for the faith.

Cowards found courage, the confused found clarity. By shaping their lives around Jesus, even in spite of their failures, this team changed the world for the better. And the truth is that we are here as disciples of Jesus in the twenty-first century because of what they did in the first century. They did it without Facebook, Twitter, Instagram, or even a flat screen TV. They did it by following the self-sacrificing, other-directed way of Jesus, by reorienting their lives around him and his teaching.

## The Movement Goes On

That's how they became a movement, the first wave of the Jesus Movement. In his book on the faith and theology of the civil rights movement, Charles Marsh of the University of Virginia at one point wrote: "Jesus had founded the most revolutionary movement in human history: a movement built on the unconditional love of God for the world and the mandate to live that love."[9] That movement has continued to surge forth just when we needed it most, just when it seemed the way of selfishness and hatred had won.

The civil rights battle for Birmingham was one of the bloodiest of the civil rights movement. It was in Birmingham that four little girls were killed when a Ku Klux Klan bomb detonated at 16th Street Baptist Church. It was in Birmingham that America saw Bull Connor unleash German Shepherd police dogs and firehoses on peaceful, nonviolent demonstrators.

As part of their training in the discipline of nonviolence, civil rights activists were given what we might call a little Rule of Life on a card. They studied it in meetings and took it with them as they marched and sat and suffered and struggled. It included these admonitions:

---

9. Marsh, 81.

- Remember the nonviolent movement seeks justice and reconciliation—not victory
- Walk and talk in the manner of love; for God is love
- Pray daily to be used by God that all men and women might be free
- Sacrifice personal wishes that all might be free
- Observe with friend and foes the ordinary rules of courtesy
- Perform regular services for others and the world
- Refrain from violence of fist, tongue, and heart
- Strive to be in good spiritual and bodily health

But the pledge began with these words:

- As you prepare to march, meditate on the life and teachings of Jesus.

Of all the preparation these movement leaders and activists could take up, nothing was more powerful than getting centered on Christ. His way—the way of sacrificial, non-self-centered love, the way of the cross, the way of nonviolent engagement—could shift and heal something fundamental in this world.

I believe in the practice of evangelism because I believe that folk committed to the Way of Jesus, the Jesus Movement, have changed the world before and can do it again. I believe things don't have to be the way they often are.

Jesus came to change the world, by the power of God's love. Love that is like what Mahatma Gandhi taught us—*satyagraha*, truth force, soul force, the force and power that can change the course of history. Truth force, soul force, the force and power that can move mountains. Jesus has shown us the way of love. And that way of love will liberate us all.

## QUESTIONS FOR THE ROAD . . .

1. On p. 14, Curry says the opposite of love is not hate but selfishness. Why might this be?

2. Review the principles for nonviolent civil rights activists on p. 18. Which do you find the most compelling for your own life and practice?

# Chapter 3

# People of the Dream

When I was a little boy I learned the words of this poem by Langston Hughes in Sunday school.

> Hold fast to dreams
> For if dreams die
> Life is a broken-winged bird
> That cannot fly.
>
> Hold fast to dreams
> For when dreams go
> Life is a barren field
> Frozen with snow.[10]

God has a dream. If God didn't, we wouldn't be here. Think about how the Bible begins with these incredible words from the ancient Hebrew poet: "In the beginning when God created the heavens and the earth, the earth was a formless void and darkness covered the face of the deep, while a wind from God swept over

---

10. *The Collected Poems of Langston Hughes: Vintage Classics,* ed. Arnold Rampersad (New York: Knopf Publishing, 1994), 32.

the face of the waters. Then God said, 'Let there be light'; and there was light" (Gen. 1:1–3).

Thus begins the process of creation, and God is the source and the author of it all. Surely when God said, "Let there be," God had something in mind. God didn't create the world and us out of sheer boredom. God had and has a dream.

God has a dream for the world God has made, for every man, woman, and child who ever has and ever will walk upon the face of the earth. God has a dream for you and a dream for me. God has a dream for this Church, for the peoples of the earth, for the entire creation. Life is meant to be lived in harmony with God's dream and vision for life and creation. When it is, life works. And when it is not, it simply doesn't.

What do we know of God's dream? Scripture lays it out in page after page, story after story. The summary isn't going to surprise you by now: in the beginning, middle, and end, it's all about love. God is love, and God created in order to share more love, to spread the love of the Trinity around in an even bigger circle, to shape and fill the whole creation with it. God welcomes us to be creatures made in the image of our creator, human beings who share in the loving, liberating, and life-giving way of the God who made us.

This is my picture of what God's dream looks like. It also matches what our own Book of Common Prayer says is the mission of the church (and what is the church but the group 100 percent dedicated to living as God's dream?). This gem is hidden in the catechism on page 855 of the 1979 Book of Common Prayer:

Q: What is the mission of the church?

A: The mission of the church is to restore all people to unity with God and each other in Christ. [11]

---

11. The Book of Common Prayer (New York: Church Publishing, 1979), 855 (hereafter BCP).

Leaders from my staff, the House of Deputies, and the General Convention sat with these words and found in them the key to the Jesus Movement. They inspired us to craft the summary I shared in chapter 1, which I think also serves as a summary of God's dream: "The Jesus Movement: Following Jesus into loving, liberating, life-giving relationship with God, with each other, and with creation." God created and then came among us in the person of Jesus of Nazareth to show us the way to be reconciled and right with God and with each other and with everything God has created. None left out. None shut out as enemies. None broken and tossed on the side. All of us beloved. All of us reconciled. That's the dream.

## The Baptized: Marked as Christ's Own Forever

It is not an accident that Matthew begins his Gospel with the genealogy of Jesus, a family tree, and then ends the Gospel with Jesus commissioning his disciples to go into the world and create a family made up of all kinds of people, born not of biology, but of baptism, and formed not by the whims of the culture, but by the teachings of Jesus.

Have you been baptized? If your answer is yes, then you were baptized into the movement led by Jesus of Nazareth. It's the movement of those committed to living out the dream of God.

> As many of you as were baptized into Christ have clothed your-selves with Christ. There is no longer Jew or Greek, there is no longer slave or free, there is no longer male and female; for all of you are one in Christ Jesus. And if you belong to Christ, then you are Abraham's offspring, heirs according to the promise. (Gal. 3:27–29)

The unity of the body of Christ is a reflection of God's vision for the unity of the human family: women and men; children and elders; rich and poor. Nobody is on the sidelines of the Jesus Movement. Or, as Elisabeth Schüssler Fiorenza explains it, God's

The unity of the body of Christ is a reflection of God's vision for the unity of the human family. Nobody is on the sidelines of the Jesus Movement.

"future is mediated and promised to all members of Israel. No one is exempted. Everyone is invited. Women as well as men, prostitutes as well as Pharisees."[12]

Not everybody was exactly on board for that kind of openness in the very beginning. It took the first council of the Church, the Council of Jerusalem, recorded in the fifteenth chapter of the Acts of the Apostles, to work out this essential pillar of our faith.

They made a decision that Gentiles could and should be included in the family of Jesus. If they were willing to follow the way of Jesus, by the power of his Spirit, then the other requirements that were laid on Jewish folk were not necessary.

I haven't had my DNA tested, but I don't think I'm Jewish. I'm pretty sure I descend from Gentile stock. That means I'm here today because of that decision to include people like me. It means the dream of God was bigger than any of our religious or tribal conditions and affiliations. The way of Jesus creates room and space for all who truly seek. That family bond stretches across all Christians, across every follower of Jesus of Nazareth. In baptism, we're marked as the people who belong to him and to each other.

## Neighbors in a New Society

If only it would stop there! But being in his family automatically means you're signed up to seek to love and serve in his spirit and in his way. When the king of the world says in Matthew 25, "I was hungry and you gave me food . . . I was a stranger and you welcomed me . . . Just as you did it to one of the least of these . . .

---

12. Elisabeth Schüssler Fiorenza, *In Memory of Her: A Feminist Theological Reconstruction of Christian Origins: Tenth Edition* (New York: Crossroad Publishing, 1994), 121.

you did it to me," that matches right up with our baptismal promise to "seek and serve Christ in all persons."[13] And when he says, "Love the Lord your God . . . , [and] love your neighbor as yourself" (Matt. 22: 37, 39), it sits alongside our baptismal promise to go about this world "loving your neighbor as yourself."[14] Faith in Jesus, following him, leads to a new way of being together. Jesus came to show us the way to become not simply the human race, not simply a gathering of tribes and kinship circles. He leads us to form a wider circle, a new society, the beloved community, the human family of God.

I began my ordained ministry serving a congregation in Winston Salem, North Carolina, in the 1970s. In the early 1980s my wife and I moved to serve in Lincoln Heights, Ohio, just outside of Cincinnati. One day I received one of those computer-generated mailings that offered to research my family genealogy and sell me a copy of the Curry family crest.

According to the advertisement, they had done some preliminary research. It started something like this: "Michael Curry, we have traced your ancestry . . ." As I read on, they gave me quite a surprise: "We have located your ancestral home and family in Ireland." I thought to myself, "Someday I'll have to travel to Ireland to see the family. I suppose it'll be one of those 'Guess who's coming to dinner?' moments."

In 1980, I thought that was hilarious. Then, on June 26, 2007, the *New York Times* ran an article that said: "DNA studies point to a common maternal ancestor of all anatomically modern humans in Africa by at least 130,000 years ago."[15] And, more recently, the New England Genealogical Society completed some research and discovered that Barack Obama and Brad Pitt and George Bush are

---

13. BCP, 305.

14. Ibid.

15. John Noble Wilford, "The Human Family Tree Has Become a Bush with Many Branches," *New York Times* (June 26, 2007).

cousins. Hillary Clinton and John McCain are cousins. And best of all, black activist Reverend Al Sharpton and the late Senator Strom Thurmond—a notorious segregationist—are cousins.

It would seem we are indeed family. God made us that way. We are meant to live that way. Imagine if Jesus Movement people helped our neighbors to live like the true human family?

In our current political season, and really in our culture as a whole, we are facing vast and deep polarization. Rank bigotry has been enshrined in the law—this is like Jim Crow all over again—and hatred is articulated in the public sphere as if it is legitimate discourse. That's a problem. And I'm not making a Republican or Democratic statement. This has nothing to do with partisanship. This has to do with citizenship.

More than ever, we need a Christian counternarrative to this polarization, partly because very often Christianity is seen as complicit with the voices of exclusion and bigotry. We need a witness by a church like the Episcopal Church to a way of being Christian that is not complicit in the culture, but committed to following Jesus, and looking like the loving, liberating, and life-giving way of Jesus of Nazareth, and serving in the way that we see Jesus serving in the New Testament. That witness in itself is a powerful antidote to the story of narrowness, bigotry, and polarization.

I believe that this Church and people in this Church can bear that witness—Episcopalians who are Republicans and Episcopalians who are Democrats and Episcopalians with no party at all. We're people of the via media, specially equipped to gather people for reconciling conversation at the center of the storm. That's who we are. That's why we sing . . .

In Christ there is no east or west
In him no south or north
But one great fellowship of love
Throughout the whole wide earth

Join hands disciples of the faith
What e'er your race may be
Who serves my Father as his child
Is surely kin to me[16]

The song is right, and when we sing it, nothing less than our survival as the human community is at stake. We cannot continue as we have been going. Martin Luther King Jr. warned everyone who would hear that, "We came over here on different ships, but we're all in the same boat now." He also said, "We shall either learn to live together as brothers and sisters, or we shall perish together as fools. The choice is ours." We can choose to build one more wall, or we can choose to grow that fellowship of love, loving our neighbors as ourselves, serving Jesus as we meet him in others.

We can choose to build one more wall, or we can choose to grow that fellowship of love, loving our neighbors as ourselves, serving Jesus as we meet him in others.

## Solidarity with the Least of These

God's dream embraces even more. This dream calls us into new, reconciled relationship, not just with other Christians, not just with our close neighbors, but ultimately with people who are hurting the most. He sends us to share the love that created all things, the liberation and fullness of life that God intends for everyone and everything God created.

Some years ago, when I was bishop of North Carolina, I traveled to the Diocese of Botswana with Bishop Trevor Mwamba, visiting various congregations and ministries. The Mother's Union and Diocese operate several daycare centers for young children. Because of the spread of HIV/AIDS, many of the children are orphans being raised by extended family members, and many are also HIV-positive themselves.

---

16. John Oxenham, "In Christ There Is No East or West."

The last daycare center we visited was at St. Peter's Church in an impoverished section of Gaborone, the capital city. We pulled into the courtyard and were greeted by the priest, Father Andrew. He and his wife are two remarkably humble and holy people of God who have dedicated their lives to saving children in the name of Jesus. He took us to the far side of the courtyard where the children were sitting on the grass in the shade, listening to Bible stories and singing songs.

Fr. Andrew introduced us. We shared in story time and later we sang this song with the children, many of whom were orphans, some HIV-positive themselves, all desperately poor:

Jesus loves me, this I know, for the Bible tells me so.
Little ones to him belong, they are weak but he is strong.
Yes, Jesus loves me.
Yes, Jesus loves me.
Yes, Jesus loves me.
The Bible tells me so.

And with that, Father dismissed the children for playtime. Off they went, running to the playground on the other side of the courtyard. All, that is, except one little girl of maybe four or five years of age. I had noticed that she was sitting in a chair, while the other children sat on the grass. What I hadn't noticed was that she had a crutch. While the other children ran, she took the crutch in her hands, staked it in the ground and pulled herself up out of the seat to walk slowly toward the playground.

As we watched, Father Andrew said the daycare director regularly checks the neighborhood for children in need. She heard about this little girl and visited her home. Her parents had died from complications of HIV/AIDS, so her grandparents were caring for her. She herself was bedridden, a victim of polio. The grandparents allowed St. Peter's and the public health service to work with her. When she first arrived at St. Peter's, she was in a wheelchair. By the time we met her, she was walking with that crutch.

Sometimes she fell down. She got back up. As she walked, Father Andrew said: "We believe that God has something better in store for every child. And it's our job to help each child find out what that is and then live."

That's the gospel message, the dream of God, and our marching orders for the Jesus Movement. God has something better in store for this world. God has a dream for the Episcopal Church, its clergy, and its laypeople. God also has a dream for the nations and peoples of the earth. God has a dream for every man, woman, and child who dwells upon the face of this earth. Our job is to love God, to love our neighbors of every kind and condition, and to love this earth, no exceptions.

## Ministry for the Jesus Way

We take up evangelism to restore all people to love with God. We take up reconciliation to restore all people to loving relationship with each other. We start ministries that reflect the varied and glorious cultures of God's family, because that's part of how we spread the love of God and love of neighbor. We lift up the voices of young people, because they are dreaming dreams and bearing prophecies that are essential to how we love God and love neighbor. We embrace the hard work of transformation with patience and savvy, wiser than we ever imagined because now we're filled with the love of God and love of neighbor.

Then all of us, all members of the human family of God, really can partner with God to change this world from the nightmare into the dream.

## QUESTIONS FOR THE ROAD . . .

1. Throughout this chapter, Curry describes in vivid detail his understanding of the dream of God. What would you say are some of the key elements of God's dream?

2. Where do you see the deepest divisions in your community? Around race? Gender? Economic class? Age? Faith? Can you imagine even one way that a church could help to heal these fissures?

# Reflections
# on the Practice
# of Ministry in the
# Way of Jesus

# Chapter 4

# On Evangelism

## Megan Castellan

I grew up neither a fundamentalist nor an ecclesiastical exile, nor the child of either one. Yet, like the prophet Amos, I inherited a bit of both.

When I was very small, my mother began to volunteer at an AIDS hospice in Hampton, Virginia. Well, this wasn't quite the case—it was the late 1980s, and the concept of "AIDS hospice" did not yet exist. What there was, in this instance, was an old house, in the worst part of the city, that could easily be mistaken for a crack house, with all the people coming and going at all parts of the day and night.

There was a man, formerly an Episcopal priest, who had been told by his bishop to either remain closeted or renounce his vows. Jack chose to renounce, and instead of pursuing a life within the church, he chose a life without. He took an inheritance, bought this house, and began to take in dying men who had no place to go. We had to keep it secret; money, supplies, and volunteers were funneled quietly from his former colleagues. And my mother, the nurse, showed up with her two young kids in tow several times a week.

They were my friends: Arles, the grinning man who rescued a cocker spaniel he found by the side of the road, who died in the first trials for AZT; Mark, the man from Puerto Rico who had strong opinions on rugs and introduced me to Queen's "Bohemian Rhapsody"; and Jack, who dressed me in his old cassock when I declared intentions of being a nun for Halloween, and took care of everyone, never counting the cost, even when the institutional church declared him an exile, unfit for service.

I heard the gospel in church each week; I saw it at Jack's House.

Yet, in the other direction, my childhood home sat a scant forty-five-minute drive from Pat Robertson's broadcasting headquarters, and the southern Virginia epicenter of the modern political, evangelical revival.

As a result, I was well-acquainted with altar calls, salvation rallies, and pledging my allegiance to the Christian flag and to the Bible. I was used to having my friends in elementary school earnestly ask me if I had received Christ into my heart. I was used to the yawning pit of embarrassment that opened in my stomach when the Baptist preacher followed up a perfectly nice concert by asking who here hadn't been saved, and begged them to come on down, while gently swelling organ music played, and the choir hummed with feeling. I was used to stoically ignoring my best friend's concerned looks as I turned my gaze toward the front, and noticed how the lady just ahead of me had the same hairstyle as my grandmother.

I was used to all of it. And it never seemed to matter that I had attended church every week of my life since I had been born. It didn't matter that I had firm theories involving which disciple was the Smartest, the Funniest, and the Most Fun at Parties. It didn't matter that I talked to Jesus in an unending stream of consciousness, and felt him to be closer to me than anyone I had ever met in the flesh. To many of the people I grew up around, because my faith tradition didn't look, smell, or taste like theirs, because it included people they considered to be cursed by God, it didn't exist.

## This Is Evangelism?

This was what I knew of evangelism. A guilt-ridden thing that coerced in the name of God—that erased my friends at Jack's House, and declared them unclean unless they assimilated, that just seemed close to outright abuse.

I really hated evangelism.

So much so that by the time I hit high school, I no longer referred to myself as a Christian. "Christians," after all, evangelized. They handed out tracts at football games. They appeared on the news, yelling about the evils of same-sex marriage, evolution, and the lie of climate change. And most of all, they seemed to have a real problem with those who weren't like them.

That wasn't me. I didn't want anything linking me to that. I didn't know what I was, but whatever it was still meant going to church every week. It involved rewriting the sermon when I was bored at my dry-cleaning job. It involved dragging every lost and lonely friend I had home with me on the holidays, and sending off money to Broadway Cares/Equity Fights AIDS in memory of the guys at the House. But nope, I wasn't a Christian, and I certainly wasn't an evangelist.

Then, a few things happened.

In the summer of 2003, I was accepted by the Young Adult Festival to attend the last five days of General Convention. I was less than thrilled. By the time I received acceptance, news had broken of Gene Robinson's election as bishop of New Hampshire—making him the first publicly partnered gay bishop in the church—and I realized that his election would be decided while I was there. This would be a disaster, I decided. Why go and witness the same fighting that I had seen play out across the news every day of my life? I had been working hard to reconcile myself to the seeming reality that the church frequently had a hard time with what the Spirit did. Why go to a national convention and watch all that work unravel?

I went anyway.

On the day of the vote in the House of Bishops, a mentor priest of mine spotted me wandering aimlessly through the halls. "Megan, sit down," he said, doing his best I'm-in-a-spy-movie-impression. "You're going to want to see this next vote."

I sat. I prayed an anxious rosary on the links of my watch band. I watched the spouses of the bishops, in front of me, pass scissors and knitting implements down the row as their spouses spoke and listened. And I held my breath in silence as the whole room prayed.

When the vote was announced, and Robinson was cleared to be consecrated a bishop, Presiding Bishop Frank Griswold led us all in prayer. We sang "Ubi Caritas," and I stumbled out into the hall, past a cluster of reporters in a daze, feeling like the world had flipped around. How does one navigate a church that can listen to the Spirit? What on earth was I supposed to do with an institution that did things that I agreed with?

## A Love Worth Sharing

A few months later, I returned to college. A friend of mine was the head of the student LGBTQ group. He asked me to come and speak about what happened at Convention.

To my utter surprise, I was excited about it. I got to explain my church! My church, which had done something I was proud of! I wasn't sure why, but at that moment, I would cheerfully explain my church.

The gathered students that day were quiet. They observed my diagrams of Episcopal polity with good humor, and I explained who Bishop Robinson was. I told them about the election confirmation. I told them about sitting in the House of Bishops, and the speech of one retired bishop, who had informed the House that he had walked in

I had to tell them this good news, because I didn't think they had heard it before. Guess what? God loves you.

believing that only a "no" vote was called for. But he had prayed, and he had listened, and now he would vote "yes."

My voice broke. My eyes filled with tears. One of the young men present put his hand on my arm comfortingly. "I know. It's ok."

In that split second, looking at this young man, these other students, most of whom had told me earlier that they had grown up in some church or other but had left, at one point or another, I thought about Jack. I thought about the people who leave, when they believe that God doesn't love them, or Jesus only wants to change them. I thought about the people who just never come, because they believe that the gospel of Christ has no relation to the church they see on the news. I thought about the times the church has failed to live up to the gospel, and the many people we've lost through our own sins.

So this was why I was there. I had to go tell them. I had to go tell them that there was this place where people knew that God loved them. There was this time when the Spirit moved and the Church listened, and it meant that more people got included, instead of excluded. I had to tell them this good news, because I didn't think they had heard it before. Guess what? God loves you. And this church acts like it.

## If We Don't Tell, Who Will?

I had no expectation that they would jump up and go to church. I have no expectation that any one of them, in the years since, has become a pledging member of their local Episcopal parish. If they do, that's fantastic, but honestly, I don't quite care. I am of the firm opinion that the Good News of God's love is only that if it is shared freely, without coercion or guilt. My responding to the love of God by going to church out of gratitude and celebration is one thing; my going to church out of profound guilt because I can't possibly deserve God's love, so I had better earn it, is another.

What Jesus commanded
us in the Great Commission
is to *not* keep this good
news to ourselves. Go and
tell people.

What Jesus commanded us in the Great Commission is to *not* keep this good news to ourselves. Go and tell people. Tell people that when the Spirit speaks, it is to crush dividing walls. Tell people that when the Spirit moves, it is to break chains, and to rebuild the destroyed cities. Tell people that when the Spirit blows, it is to empower the people of God to come together and stretch out their hands to welcome and include—and that despite its best efforts at times, the very institution itself can't stop it.

We have to tell them this story. Not to erase their story and not to demand something from them, but because, if we don't, others will tell a story for us. Other voices will rise up to tell a false story about what and who God is, and what God wants. Others will lie in God's name, to satisfy their own insecurity and fear, if we are silent about the faith that is in us. And countless others will go through life feeling abandoned by the Christ who gave himself for them, the God who became incarnate to be with them, and the Spirit who flows around them daily.

We have to give them words for this. We have to tell them our stories. Our stories of being loved when we were lost and alone. Our stories of having our minds changed. Our stories of finding Christ when we didn't expect it. Our stories of being confronted by a love so strong that no other story could change it.

We all have these stories—stories of when Christ became real, and the love of God changed how we saw the world. These stories need telling, because these are the stories that light up the world. These are the stories that make Jesus real.

## QUESTIONS FOR THE ROAD . . .

**1.** Castellan shares the story of her misgivings about evangelism, and how she overcame them. Do you have any negative impressions about "evangelism"? What are they? Where did they come from?

**2.** The word "evangelism" is rooted in the Greek word *evangelion*, which means "good news." Is there any good news—perhaps even a story—about God that you wish other people knew? How could you share it?

# Chapter 5

# On New, Multicultural Ministries

## Anthony Guillén

"I'd rather have my church burn than let those Mexicans in," a small-statured, properly dressed church woman hissed at me.

I had been told this dying congregation was interested in exploring Latino/Hispanic ministry, so I arrived with PowerPoint presentation in hand to share all sorts of data about changes in our country. For instance, the Census Bureau projects the United States population will increase 42 percent by 2050. That includes a 167 percent increase in the Latino/Hispanic population, 142 percent among Asian people, a 56 percent increase among black people, and 1 percent growth of the white population. Already, the United States is the second largest Latino/Hispanic country in the world.

I shared these facts with missionary zeal, and part of me expected cries of "Hallelujah" at this revelation of the great evangelistic opportunity at this church's doorstep.

Instead, my sister in Christ spoke those words: "I'd rather have my church burn than let those Mexicans in." Never mind that her church was preparing to pronounce last rites. She spoke from a place of total fear, maybe a fear that other faithful Episcopalians feel, but dare not utter. And she made me wonder: How much do we fear the immigrant, the foreigner, anyone who does not resemble those already in "our" church? How much do we fear discovering something new about ourselves?

These fears are prevalent in seemingly every society, but they are not what the Jesus Movement is all about. We are a movement of love, acceptance, and inclusivity, a movement that calls for both evangelism and reconciliation. With growing ethnic communities in just about every city and town in the United States, the Episcopal Church could practice both at the same time.

As Director of Ethnic Ministries for the Episcopal Church Center, and as Missioner for Latino/Hispanic Ministries, I partner with the Offices of Asiamerica Ministries, Black Ministries, and Indigenous Ministries, all of whom also work closely with the team responsible for New Church Starts and Missional Initiatives. Everywhere you look, Episcopalians are planting new churches, redeveloping existing congregations, developing leaders, and discovering the gift of ethnic ministry. In this moment, nearly every Episcopal Church could be engaged in some form of multicultural ministry.

## The Many Facets of Asian Ministry

Signs of hope are emerging everywhere. Asiamerica and Pacific Islanders ministries in the Episcopal Church are among the most diverse and pan-ethnic of ministries. The Reverend Canon Winfred Vergara is staff missioner for this area, uniting ministry in seven ethnic groups: Chinese, Japanese, Korean, Filipino, South Asian, Southeast Asian, and Pacific Islander churches in the United States, and the many nations where our church is present (including Taiwan and Micronesia). The ministries link with new Asian immigrants, with Asian Americans, and with Anglican and ecumenical churches in Asia. The joy and challenge of serving at this intersection is like mining diamonds with many facets.

In this moment, nearly every Episcopal Church could be engaged in some form of multicultural ministry.

Except for the Philippines (which is 92 percent Christian, mainly Roman Catholic) and South Korea (which is 33 percent evangelical Christian), most Asians come from non-Christian backgrounds. As a result, Episcopal Asian ministry is inevitably a ministry of dialogue with people of other faiths, cultures, and ideologies, such as Japanese immigrants who hail from Shinto backgrounds, South Asians rooted in Hinduism, Sikh, or Muslim traditions, and Southeast Asians shaped by Buddhist backgrounds, along with new immigrants from China with Communist ideological orientations. Asian ministry provides a rich missional opportunity beyond the racial and cultural confines of the Episcopal Church.

Holy Apostles in St. Paul, Minnesota, took that mission challenge seriously. The mostly European-American church had diminished, and The Rev. Bill Bulson was sent to help the congregation to embrace a good death. Unbeknownst to him, there was a nearby Hmong community destined to change Holy Apostles.

The Hmong are mountain farmers from China and Laos, with no country of their own. During the Vietnam War they were allies of the United States, and after the war, they were in danger of genocide. To survive, they repatriated to the United States, and many settled in Minnesota. This particular Hmong group was worshipping at the Roman Catholic Church in St. Paul, but they had experienced ostracism and were seeking a new place to gather and celebrate their faith.

Bulson learned of their plight and offered Holy Apostles's facilities. He thought perhaps fifty or so people would show up; to his surprise, five hundred people arrived to worship. What began as a simple hospitable invitation soon turned into a robust ministry with a community eager to accept this new spiritual home.

The Hmong community was officially welcomed into Holy Apostles parish in 2005. In one historic service, three hundred Hmong were confirmed and received into the Episcopal Church—it took three bishops and a three-hour service to accomplish this feat. The ministry continued to take root, and soon lay leader Toua Vang was sent to Virginia Theological Seminary in Alexandria. He was ordained as the first Hmong priest. Since then, four more Hmong priests have been ordained.

Holy Apostles now serves as the training center for new Hmong ministries, sharing wisdom with a wider church hungry to learn about ministry across cultural borders.

## The Amazing Grace of Black Ministries

Enslaved and free, Northern and Southern, rich and poor—black people have been part of the Episcopal Church since it arrived on these shores. Today, Black Ministries in the Episcopal Church embraces African Americans and people of African descent from the Caribbean, South and Latin America, as well as expatriates from Africa, many of whom have escaped civil unrest in their countries of origin. That particular ministry on the margins has been close to the heart of The Rev. Canon Angela Ifill, who served more than a decade as Missioner for Black Ministries. She shared this story of the grace and life-giving power of Episcopal black ministries:

In 2001 the United Nations High Commissioner for Refugees began cooperating with U.S. officials to resettle the Lost Boys of Sudan, orphaned children displaced by their country's civil war. Many of these Lost Boys were part of the Episcopal Church of Sudan and naturally sought Episcopal churches once they settled in the United States. In most instances they were allowed to hold late afternoon worship services, but they were rarely invited to participate in the worship or fellowship of the host congregation. Sadly many of these so-called Lost Boys were lost to us—they left the Episcopal Church and went to other, more welcoming denominations.

Ifill gathered thirty or so of these young men to learn how the Episcopal Church could better partner with them. She listened to their stories, including one who told her, "Everyone calls us the Lost Boys—but we're not lost—we have Jesus." Many were convinced that Jesus had brought them to this place. "Our mission here is to be missionaries for this church," another young man said.

They did not wait for their host church to save them. Instead, they began to imagine how they could support one another, and more importantly, support churches that might want to minister with them. They drew up lists of existing communities and leaders, and determined their numbers reached thousands in some forty Episcopal dioceses. They worked to alert various dioceses of their presence and of their desire to unite with host churches and with their peers who felt displaced. From these seeds they grew the Sudanese Leadership Institute for Learning and Advancement, which provides training for leaders in their communities and assists with the integration of their local congregations.

In 2012, Sudanese ministry leaders were invited for the first time to attend General Convention in Indianapolis, a major turning point in the ministry's development. They returned to Convention in 2015, this time with proposals for developing sustainable ministry over the long haul. The Lost Boys said they now felt connected and received within the life of the church. They had a place in the Jesus Movement too.

## New Life through Latino Ministry

As the Episcopal Church's Missioner for Latino/Hispanic Ministries, I learn every day from entrepreneurial clergy and members who serve the Jesus Movement in the United States and throughout Latin America. It takes faith and courage for these communities of color to show up and be heard in the Episcopal Church, given the fear and racism that shape so much of life.

Our aim is to embody a peace whose power breaks down divisions that keep us apart (Eph. 2:14). We see a beautiful spiritual home in the Episcopal Church, and we are willing to persevere and build relationships in order to secure it.

Why do Latinos keep the faith? Our aim is to embody a peace whose power breaks down divisions that keep us apart (Eph. 2:14). Many of us see a beautiful spiritual home in the Episcopal Church, and we are willing to persevere and build relationships in order to secure it. I see leaders embodying that reconciling spirit across the Episcopal Church.

In the fall of 2006, The Rev. Vidal Rivas began his ministry with a Latino congregation based at a mostly white Episcopal Church in greater Washington, DC. The Latino group was only a few years old, with few members, but it soon grew in number *and* in spiritual depth. In one year, Rivas had prepared and presented twenty-seven adults to be received into the Episcopal Church.

The host congregation, alarmed by this growth and by Vidal's involvement in the community, labeled him a "revolutionary." Eventually, the rector and vestry asked the Latinos in their midst to find a new home. Half of the congregation left the Episcopal Church in response to this rejection, but those who remained eventually found a new home at St. Matthews in Hyattsville, Maryland.

St. Matthews was a fledging congregation renting space to a Methodist congregation to make ends meet. Vidal and his thirty-one members arrived at St. Matthews in October 2008 and began a noon service sandwiched between the 10:00 a.m. Episcopal service and the 2:00 p.m. Methodist service. Though occasional skirmishes ensued as they negotiated life together—usually complaints about the noisy and rowdy children, the number of gatherings and meals, and of course the bilingual services—overall the people of St. Matthews were warm and hospitable. Maybe God could do more with them together than apart?

In 2010, the two Episcopal congregations opted to merge and form one church. In 2011, the two became one flesh, with a vestry made up of equal numbers of Latinos and whites, and the rectors named as co-rectors.

By 2012, an 8:00 a.m. service that began with twelve people turned into an average attendance of eighty. The noon service that began with thirty-one grew to average between 250 and 400 people, and a newer 5:00 p.m. service had already grown to welcome 80 to 150 congregants every Sunday. Meanwhile, the Sunday school averaged 110 children.

The church has continued to evolve. Today, Rivas is the senior priest and the vestry more closely reflects the proportion of Latinos in the congregation. There is a fear across the wider church that Latino membership equals a drop in giving. Instead, at St. Matthews, Latinos now pledge and give more than their white counterparts. The goal is not to replace white members with different cultures, but I am inspired as I see people of every race fully expressing love for the God in whose image we were all created. That is happening in Hyattsville and beyond.

## Diversity and the Dream of God

In Revelation 5:9–10, we see a vision of the saints from "every tribe and language and people and nation" singing a song of praise before the throne of the Lamb of God. The passage makes clear that this is God's intention for the future of the worshipping community and for all humanity. The Spirit of God leads us to embrace multicultural, multilingual, multiethnic relationship.

Of course, if we look at the present age, we are far from God's intention for humanity. Still, we take the risk and draw near one another. The intimacy brings some conflict. It also awakens us to see and celebrate the beauty of God's hope for humanity. The church must be the "first fruits" of this dream, the one community where people see a glimpse of God's preferred future. This is the direction of the Jesus Movement.

## QUESTIONS FOR THE ROAD . . .

**1.** If you're part of an Episcopal Church, have a look at the census data for the area near your church. (See the data at www.episcopalchurch.org/evangelism, under "Church and Neighborhood Demographics.") Now compare the racial and ethnic make-up of your church's general area with the composition of your congregation. What do you notice? Feel free to expand the circle to diverse areas adjacent to your church. With what communities could your church be engaged in relationship?

**2.** One woman said she would rather see her church burn than welcome "Mexicans." How would you respond to someone who views diversity in this way?

**3.** Have you ever seen groups crossing racial and cultural lines in a way that looks like the Jesus Movement to you? Describe it now.

# Chapter 6

# On Ministry with and by Young Adults

Kellan Day

For the last few decades, research and statistics have kept churches anxious about the dwindling young adult population. Like the Israelites, we have grumbled and stumbled along, complaining that our churches are shrinking and subtly blaming God—or young adults—for bringing us to this place.

That is a strong temptation. Thankfully, we do not need to live in constant fear of who will occupy our churches twenty or even fifty years down the road. We can be assured the Jesus Movement will not shrivel to nothing. Evangelism and subsequent discipleship does not come instantly, but they can come as we trust where the Spirit guides us.

Make no mistake: God has shown up and God will continue to transform churches, communities, and lives. I find it helpful to recall the stories of that abundance and generosity, especially as I have seen it among young adults.

## We Yearn for Tradition

I remember my own introduction to the Episcopal branch of the Jesus Movement. It began most unexpectedly: a group of young adults in Grand Rapids, Michigan, wandered into an Episcopal Church. We sat alone and left quickly following the Benediction. Intrigued but not yet convinced of this new-to-us expression of faith, we kept our distance and just experienced the liturgy. The oddness and oldness of it slowly worked their subconscious magic: drawing us in, pulling at both our bodies and our spirits, syncing us with an ancient pattern of observing time and seasons. Some of us even began to call ourselves Episcopalians.

Perhaps the old-time congregants asked themselves, "Who are these young people?" and "Why do they keep showing up for worship on Sunday morning?" Many of us grew up in nondenominational, Reformed, and Bible churches, where our faith tended to hinge on ever-changing and now fleeting feelings. When we grew out of our adolescence, it seemed we also grew out of our faith. We longed for God, but could not find God on our own.

When the Episcopal Church gave us the space to explore mystery rather than feign certainty, it was like receiving a warm drink on a winter's night. As we started to practice our faith in this nourishing context, we discovered the richness of tradition and catholicity (a church that is broad and seeks to express the faith in many contexts). And more young adults continued to join us.

Eventually there was a large enough young adult cohort in Grand Rapids that we could get organized. Our diocese applied for a grant, and that money catalyzed the diocesan commitment to a young adult missioner position. Thus began our young adult community experiment.

## We Yearn for Community

The community met every Thursday evening; we cooked together and prayed together and discussed Jean Vanier's *Community and*

*Growth.* Throughout the first season of the experiment, our friendships grew, as did our sense of commitment.

The original leader was a gifted and charismatic leader with a special knack for visioning and persuading. He dreamed of a young adult group that would, over time, evolve into its own worshipping community modeled after the Fresh Expressions movement in England, which sought to express ancient Anglican traditions in fresh ways that met changing contexts. His dream was to bring in scholars one night of the week, host a round-table discussion on art another night, carry on our typical Evensong liturgy on yet another evening, and (not surprisingly) have a weekly "Theology on Tap" event with beer and Bible out in public. This Christian community would invest in the neighborhood, till the gardens, feed and house anyone who was in need.

> The Fresh Expressions movement in England sought to express ancient Anglican traditions in fresh ways that met changing contexts.

It was a glorious image of God's dream. I know communities that have pursued something like it, and they have thrived. But it didn't necessarily match the yearning or capacity of our particular young adult community. Many of us were moving in and out of new homes and new jobs in new places; we could not commit our whole lives to this experiment. Most of us participated because we were looking for friends, a warm meal, and a praying community in the relationally barren tundra of post-college life.

More importantly, many of the young adults in the community were connected to and deeply loved parish life with its intergenerational community. As easy as it would be to only hang with people in our demographic, we knew it would be spiritually and relationally constricting. We owed our faith to loving mentors and parents and professors back home. Why would we want to leave those life-defining relationships for a community of solely young adults, especially when we saw people our own age throughout the week?

Christian Smith—the well-regarded sociologist on American youth and religion—has pointed to intergenerational relationships as the number one factor for whether or not young people stay involved in their religious communities. We could all use some intergenerational accountability.

At the same time, we want to listen to and bless our young adult peers. We all have plenty of friends who are moving away from the church, purposefully and accidentally. Each person's situation may be different. One friend simply stopped believing in God after taking a few biology courses in college. Another didn't like the social anxiety that accompanied Sunday morning. Yet another was so idealistic about church he was dissatisfied with the reality of ecclesial and communal life.

To hastily pull these friends back to the institutional church misses the point. We love the church, we love our friends, and we're committed to honoring the integrity of both groups. It was important to the Jesus Movement that we keep traveling and sharing in both worlds.

## We Yearn for What the World Cannot Give

After six months in this young adult community experiment, the community reached a crossroads and the young adult missioner left. We fumbled along for a few months, lost and leaderless, until we realized we needed help.

Poet David Whyte urges us to stop the conversation in times of desolation or wandering. Return to silence, seek God, and then you may have something worthwhile to say. Through the power of the Spirit and the help of Sister Ann, a Dominican nun who became our companion, we discerned that each young adult was wholeheartedly committed to the community project.

It's important to note that what worked for us isn't a recipe for every ministry with or by young adults. Our vision reflected the specific character and hopes of our assembly. For instance, most of us were committed both to our young adult weekly gatherings *and* to our respective home parishes. We found Jesus on Sunday mornings, and we wouldn't have missed the Eucharist for any-thing. As the Rev. Beth Maynard put it in her essay on young adults in the late 1990s: "You can pretty much count on the fact that if [young adults] are [in church], it's because we want some-thing not so easily found anywhere else: a living God and a spiri-tual community."[17] And what we've discovered is that the gospel is the most magnificent story to ever be heard, the most beautiful way to participate in this world.

In my experience, there is no need to specially package the gospel; just preach it. There is no need to remove the traditional or more "spiritual" elements from young adult gatherings; we ache for it. We didn't come to the Episcopal Church because it was flashy or up-to-date—far from it. We came because it is an ancient and life-giving tradition that feeds our souls and bodies. Or as preacher Jonathan Martin puts it: "I went out of sheer, bold-faced desperation for someone to preach the gospel to me, someone to lay hands on me, and someone to offer me the Lord's Supper. There was no motivation more noble than hoping to not starve."[18]

More often than not, the world offers empty calories, insisting that we consume a flashy and marketable experience. What we found in Episcopal community, as young adults, is so small and mundane, it might just be the work of the Spirit.

## We Yearn to Follow Jesus

We are seeking to be good Christians in the world, in our specific communities. At church we learn how to not just be good Chris-

---

17. Beth Maynard, "ISO Peer Group: Episcopal Culture through an Xers Lens," in *Gathering the NeXt Generation: Essays on the Formation and Ministry of GenX Priests*, ed. Nathan Humphrey (Harrisburg, PA: Morehouse Publishing, 2000), 83.

18. John Martin, "On Going to (an Episcopal) Church," *Medium*, January 6, 2015, https://medium.com/@theboyonthebike/on-going-to-an-episcopal-church-428781564139#.y91j56eu6.

What we found, as young adults who discovered our place in the Jesus Movement, is that it all begins with Jesus.

tians but how to be more fully human. Jesus teaches us how to be fully human in his wry stories and beloved Beatitudes. It is from this starting point, knowing and seeking Jesus, that we are able to effectively evangelize and seek reconciliation in all places of brokenness. What we found, as young adults who discovered our place in the Jesus Movement, is that it all begins with Jesus.

We didn't want to start a movement that others could model a program after, and swell the ranks of parishes nationwide. What we wanted was to belong to a body of disciples—to make some friends, to share our faith over a meal, and to pray honestly and consistently.

Sometimes—perhaps most of the time—the Jesus Movement gets lived out in ministries and stories that are not raging successes. Instead, the movement gains momentum slowly. Look at the haphazard community of Jesus's disciples from the beginning. If the data on religion in America is right, we should get used to this kind of rocky road to the kingdom. Our budgets will be cut and our buildings will continue to deteriorate. Fear and self-recrimination and competitive instincts will likely cause more suffering.

But we cannot succumb to those forces. Jesus tells Martha in Luke 10:42 that there is "need of only one thing." Christians gather and pray in our Lord's name, eat with one another, love our enemies, and tend the garden. It is what we do. This "one thing" will outlast the decrepit buildings and the outdated programming. This "one thing" will welcome and grow new Christians of new generations, who seek authentic and meaningful connection to God, to each other, and to our elders.

As long as we are doing the hard and healing work of the gospel, the Jesus Movement will move ahead. Young adults join all Christians in this movement because we have so much to learn—and so much to share—and because we, too, want to follow Jesus.

## QUESTIONS FOR THE ROAD . . .

**1.** Are you part of a church or ministry? If so, are young adults present and engaged? How could you "stop the conversation" and actively seek relationship with more young adults (including if you are a young adult yourself)?

**2.** Think about a moment when intergenerational relationships enhanced your faith. When did someone older or someone younger draw you closer to God? What happened?

# Chapter 7

# On Racial Reconciliation and Justice

## Broderick Greer

Following the 2014 murder of teenager Michael Brown by officer Darren Wilson in Ferguson, Missouri, Christians of various denominations and races called on the Church to engage in the work of racial reconciliation. These followers of Christ drew on texts of Scripture, tradition, personal experience, and recent social movements to issue this faithful, if vague, invitation. "The way forward," the mantra went, "involves Christians—black, white, etc.—laying aside what divides us and a willingness to meet at the table of reconciliation." As I heard these platitudes, I grew increasingly concerned.

At the time of Michael Brown's murder, I was a twenty-four-year-old senior at Virginia Theological Seminary, being formed for priestly ordination in the Episcopal Church. I had a sense that the reconciliation so many well-meaning Christians lauded was merely a nod to the substantive prophetic and apostolic demands of reconciliation placed on the people of God in the sacrament of baptism. I am more convinced than ever that there must be more to racial reconciliation than black and white church pulpit swaps and church administrative tokenism, especially when the circumstances that lead to this desire for reconciliation are nothing new. Racism suffocates the "loving, liberating, and life-giving" way of the Jesus Movement. Concern for and engagement with the suffering of oppressed populations must be wedded to the liberating nature of the baptized life. A part of this work of love and liberation is discussing the complicity of the Episcopal Church and broader white majority of American Christianity in racism and other social sins—and determining how we can practice a way of life that establishes true justice and reconciliation.

## Two Christianities

White American Christianity has played a prominent role in the genesis and reinforcement of our nation's racialized social order. For centuries, white churches used the Doctrine of Discovery to justify the cultural erasure of indigenous peoples. For nearly as long, white American Christians have used the Bible to justify the inhumane treatment of black people, beginning with biblical interpretations that asserted that black people bore the Curse of Ham (Gen. 9), explaining that black people were prime candidates for enslavement. Post–Civil War, this interpretation evolved into white Christians arguing that the divine social order demanded the races remain separate, a reality that remains in the United States, given that schools are as racially segregated today as they were in 1968.[19]

Meanwhile, as white Christians were using Christianity to exclude or demoralize black people, black Christians were creating—in ingenious ways—communities of belonging and songs of resistance. At one Thursday night choir rehearsal in the black church

---

19. See http://www.pbs.org/wgbh/frontline/article/a-return-to-school-segregation-in-america/.

of my childhood, my maternal grandmother, Faerie, taught us this song for the movement:

> We've met jail and violence, too
> But God's love will see us through
> Keep your eyes on the prize
> Hold on, hold on.

Jail, violence, enslavement, and white supremacist interpretations of Christianity could not and cannot quell the Spirit of liberation inhabiting God's black children.

Over the past few years, black people have taken to the streets of America's towns and cities from Ferguson to Baltimore, New York City to Oakland, to dramatize their dissatisfaction with the racist status quo, even as Native people have resisted the desecration of land, water, and sacred sites protected by the Standing Rock Sioux Tribe. The moment in which we live is too urgent—too many lives lost, dreams deferred, and nightmares realized—to commit ourselves to anything but whole-hearted "reconciliation."

## A Matter of Time

In an interview about her work around concepts of time in Native American mythology and storytelling, poet and author Leslie Marmon Silko says, "If time is round, if time is an ocean, then something that happened 500 years ago may be quite immediate and real, whereas something inconsequential that happened an hour ago could be far away." She goes on to say, "I grew up among people whose experience of time is a bit different. In their sense of time, 500 years is not a far distance, and that's why there is no need for the reinterpretation."[20]

---

20. Thomas Irmer and Matthias Schmidt, "An Interview with Leslie Marmon Silko (1995)," in *Conversations with Leslie Marmon Silko* (Jackson, Mississippi: University of Mississippi Press, 2000), 149.

In other words, social trauma is never something that happened a "long time ago," but is a very real fissure, even in the lives of those who did not experience the trauma in first person. When a Michael Brown or a Rekia Boyd is killed and their stories get a bit of media air time, the first thing many people think is that these are isolated events, that this a new phenomenon, that police terrorizing black bodies is a "new" thing. There is nothing new about white violence in the United States.

As Silko implies, time can be used in violent, linear ways. Because the dominant culture is, in some way, bound to frame its own history of oppressing others as a series of unrelated events, it is easier to convince today's oppressed that their oppression is not tied to the oppression of the past. White supremacy is reinforced when the public is convinced that mass incarceration and the so-called "War on Drugs" is not in continuity with the enslavement of black people from 1619 to 1865, or that economic reparations for black enslavement are not due to living African Americans.

White supremacy is reinforced when it is convinced there is no curvature to time. And yet, the blood of thousands of Native and black Americans cry to us from the ground, pleading with us to remember that their deaths are part of the vast ocean of American history; that their deaths occurred in the ongoing dialogue between violent, unchecked white supremacy and the lives of black and Native people in the United States.

## Whither Reconciliation?

When American Christians use the word "reconciliation" in terms of the history of abuse of black Americans by white Americans, there is an implication that two sides are guilty in ongoing racial oppression, even though newspaper headlines, school-to-prison statistics, and police brutality tell a different story. If white Americans continue to convince themselves that "racial tension"—and not anti-black racism—is the source of this nation's woes, their participation in actual reconciliation will continue to be deluded and ineffective.

Any discussion of reconciliation that is faithful to the Good News of God in Christ is one that is unafraid of naming the reality of power dynamics. If a person is abused by their spouse for years and the spouse repeatedly apologizes, but never names the wrong done or concrete measures they will take to reorient the way they will treat their spouse, we would call that abuse. In the same way, if white American Christians readily apologize, but refuse to address underlying issues of racial terror and discrimination and the specific ways they will work to dismantle white supremacy, it is abuse.

When I have discussed reconciliation in this way before, I have regularly been met with curious statements like, "But God doesn't demand works or reparations before being reconciled to us," and I do not disagree. One of the most freeing aspects of the baptized life is that there are no prerequisites to God loving and forgiving us once-and-for-all. Anything less than that reality is an affront to the grace of God. And yet, forgiveness is neither a forgetting of wrongdoing nor a free pass toward further abuse, but an invitation toward lifelong reorientation.

## Turning to the Jesus Way Every Day

Episcopal Christians are uniquely positioned for this kind of lifelong reorientation, given the way we understand conversion. Instead of seeing conversion as a singular moment in time, followers of Jesus in the Episcopal Way understand that the project of reorientation launched in baptism unfolds over a lifetime, with a gradual compounding of disappointments, victories, missteps, and resurrections. If we didn't see personal reorientation and repentance as a day-by-day process, we wouldn't confess our sins daily, as we do in both the Daily Office and Holy Eucharist. And if lifelong, personal reorientation toward love is something we're committed to, then so is lifelong, social reorientation. After all, as public theologian Cornel West has said, "Justice is what love looks like in public."[21]

As our knowledge of the current environmental crisis reaches new depths, one would find it laughable to suggest that environmental healing is a simple, linear project. Instead, people serious about offsetting irreversible damage done by humans to creation over the last 150 years recognize the dynamism and diversity of the challenges we and our forebears have imposed on what the prayer book calls "this fragile earth, our island home."[22]

The same is true when it comes to our discussion of ending white supremacy and other forms of social violence. The inequalities waged against black Americans by white Americans from 1619 onward cannot be completely reversed in my or my children's lifetimes. The social, economic, and psychological damage done to women, Native, black, LGBTQ, and other American populations in the name of white supremacy, misogyny, and heterosexism is irreversible, but that reality needn't paralyze God's Easter people. Why? Because, as theologian James Cone has written: "God took the evil of the cross and the lynching tree and transformed them both into the triumphant beauty of the divine. If America has the courage to confront the great sin and ongoing legacy of white supremacy with repentance and reparation there is hope 'beyond tragedy.'"[23]

Existing "beyond tragedy" means recognizing and practicing the transformative power of reconciliation and forgiveness in-

---

21. "Cornel West Talks to David Shuster," Al Jazeera-America, February 24, 2014, http://america.aljazeera.com/watch/shows/talk-to-al-jazeera/interviews-and-more/2014/2/24/cornel-west-talkstodavidshuster.html.

22. BCP, 370.

23. James Cone, *The Cross and the Lynching Tree* (Maryknoll, NY: Orbis Books, 2011), 66.

formed by the Paschal Mystery. In his resurrection, Jesus does not scold the apostle
Peter; instead he recommissions him, beg-
ging him to "feed my sheep" (John 21:17).
In the process, Jesus shows us that forgiveness holds potential as a means toward a re-
storative future, one in which God's reality
of wholeness breaks into ours. Following
Jesus, we can recognize the tragedies of our

> Following Jesus, we can recognize the tragedies of our present age, understand them for what they are, and allow them to influence our lifelong journey toward the New Jerusalem.

present age, understand them for what they are, and allow them to
influence our lifelong journey toward the New Jerusalem, a place
and time when every tribe, nation, and language celebrates God's
wondrous deeds in their native tongue and in their native land.

Existing "beyond tragedy" means exchanging synthetic forms
of reconciliation that erase the scars of Jesus's lynching in resurrection for the weighty reality of the risen Christ retaining the
scars of his crucifixion. There is an honesty about Jesus's post-
resurrection body, a boldness that addresses his pain, but doesn't
end with it; a sign that God is not interested in premature healing.
This honesty—of naming traumas, scars, and other messy aspects
of human experience—must be present in the Episcopal Church's
commitment to offsetting anti-black racism in our time and in
generations to come.

In terms of a social project as sweeping and horrific as white
supremacy, reconciliation cannot happen without reparations, seeing as it is impossible to reconcile a relationship that was never
conciliatory, a relationship built on the assumption that white people had and have the right to dominate people of color.

The very mention of reparations can stymie even the most
progressive conversation about race. The term implies a radical
redistribution of wealth, power, and narrative. In concrete terms,
however, it means offering whatever platforms we may have—
Sunday morning forums, Christian formation gatherings—for tra-
ditionally oppressed people to tell their stories, normalizing their

experiences in the church's life. It means stepping out from our familiar ecclesial and cultural enclaves and investing the time and resources necessary to encounter people different from ourselves.

For too long, Native and black Americans and other racial, ethnic, sexual, and gender minorities have been forced to the margins of American society, relegated to obscure footnotes in the history textbooks of our nation's schools. Racial reconciliation and justice requires white Christians interested in substantial social transformation to learn how their ancestors created and benefited from whiteness, how they themselves reinforce that identity, and how that identity has been and is used to oppress others. Only in that self-knowledge will the seeds of social wholeness be planted and begin taking root.

## QUESTIONS FOR THE ROAD . . .

1. Greer speaks honestly about two versions of Christianity: one reinforces the dominant culture and racist systems, the other heralds liberation and reconciliation. As you look at the history of Christianity and at your own experience of it, do you see moments when it has supported racism?

2. This chapter includes several suggestions for practicing reconciliation and reparation, including speaking honestly about white racism, honoring stories and strategies rising from communities of color, repenting of the sin of racism, repairing what has been broken, linking the trauma of past generations to current struggles, stepping into unfamiliar spaces, ultimately offering and receiving forgiveness. Which of these seems the most crucial to you, for the work of reconciliation?

# Chapter 8

# On Being Part of the World

## Nora Gallagher

> He put before them another parable: "The kingdom of heaven is like a mustard seed that someone took and sowed in his field; it is the smallest of all the seeds, but when it has grown it is the greatest of shrubs and becomes a tree, so that the birds of the air come and make nests in its branches." (Matt. 13:31–32)

On the last day of June, five years ago, I was making my way through the long day-before-you-leave-town list. I'd just ticked off "cat food," when the phone rang. The tone of my friend Anne's voice was enough without what followed: "Nora," she said. "Something has happened to Mark. I'm on my way to the hospital. Could you meet me there?"

I put down the list and walked out the door. And when I got to the door of the emergency room, Anne ran out and we grabbed each other and our whole bodies shook.

We sat outside at a little metal table with the fire chief and a chaplain waiting for them to bring Mark in. He had had "some kind of accident" while surfing up the coast. They were bringing him in by helicopter and an ambulance.

The ambulance drove up and a bunch of people wearing white and green hospital coats walked out with a wheeled gurney and pulled open the ambulance doors as if they were breaking through a wall. Two guys inside were already pushing the stretcher out, and I saw Mark covered in a blanket. An oxygen mask covered his mouth.

"This is not good," the chaplain whispered in my ear.

They rushed him past us and into the hospital and the doors closed.

We followed them past the reception desk, and the people in the doorways and the hallways as if they were wheat and we were threshers. Then we were inside the trauma room and there were people everywhere. One doctor barking orders, but it was quiet, orderly. It lasted a few long seconds. Then the doctor turned to Anne. He took her hands.

"This has to stop," he said. "We are not getting brain function. We need to stop."

She screamed and bent over double and I tried to gather her up in my arms, but she was too big. I could only hold her around her waist. Anne said she wanted to stay with him and they said yes and then the room was empty except for us.

Anne walked right into it; she did not duck it. I got the Kleenex and the bottled water and the cloth to wash her face. I did hardly anything, and yet my kinetic memory of that day is of being picked up and thrown against a wall and then being picked up and thrown at it again.

When you are in the midst of this kind of trauma, you need a very big story to contain it. I didn't want a page from the *Death for Dummies* textbook or a ready comfort book. I didn't see God in that room. Not anywhere. I saw a dead man and his wife, my beloved friend, sobbing on the floor holding tight to his arm. Jesus did not rescue me or Anne. If someone had told me that day that God was in the room, I would have gladly knocked her teeth out.

I knew I'd found a place big enough to sink my grief and exhaustion and fear. It was resilient and wordless and full of vitality.

I went through the rest of that week as one does: helping, cooking, gathering. I did not find God in church that Sunday. We all got through Mark's memorial. And then my husband, Vincent, and I got on a plane and finally went on vacation. We were both so tired that once we got to my cousins' cabin in the mountains, we had a big fight.

But in the morning, the air cleared. We went for a hike in the high Cascades. On our way up there, we saw a mountain goat chewing a shrub with his fur falling off him in pieces as if he were wearing a discarded rug. From a ridge trail, we could see a circle of peaks like a necklace of jagged diamonds. We walked up through lupine and columbine and icy creeks. We got to the top and smelled the den of a mountain lion. We crossed a vast snow field. In the midst of it, I knew I'd found a place big enough to sink my grief and exhaustion and fear. It was resilient and wordless and full of vitality. And it was more than that.

After a week in the mountains, my thoughts and memories of Mark's death felt as if they had been gradually whirled in a centrifuge until each had found their proper weight and place. I was more than comforted; I felt that what had been battering me from outside myself was now part of me, because I was part of a larger order.

## We Are Dust and Water

In 2015, Pope Francis published an encyclical called *Laudato Si*, or "Praise be to you, Lord." It's the first papal encyclical to be devoted solely to the environment. It's a letter to everyone, not just Catholics and not just Christians. He writes, "We have forgotten that we ourselves are dust of the earth [see Genesis 2:7]; our very bodies are made up of her elements, we breathe her air, and we receive life and refreshment from her waters."[24] Francis says that more than anything else, we need a change of heart. We need to convert. Not to Catholicism or even Christianity, but to a new relationship to what he calls our common home. A new relationship to the world.

Michael Curry reminded everyone of the significance of the waters of creation, for human life and for our relationship to God, in the fall of 2016, when he visited the Standing Rock encampment in North Dakota. At Standing Rock, the Sioux Nation gathered thousands of people to protect the waters of the Missouri River and their sacred sites from a crude oil pipeline. Curry said, "When we baptize a new follower of Jesus Christ, we pray these words over the water of baptism: 'We thank you, Almighty God, for the gift of water.'" He cited the many ways water has been used to bless and fill humanity and all of life, and begged Episcopalians to honor and "protect all other forms of life."[25]

If we think of ourselves as separate from the earth and the waters, we are lost and isolated. To be alive is to be part of the world.

A man said to me at a recent workshop: "I find God when I'm walking along a river." And then he looked embarrassed, as if he was saying something he should not say. So many people—Republicans, Democrats, Independents, hunters, fishermen and women, hikers, birders, walkers—say that where they easily find God or have an experience of the holy is in the natural world. And they, like the man who talked to me, look ill at ease when they say it, especially if they are regular churchgoers. And well they might: Christianity has a history of burning people who like the world

---

24. Pope Francis, "Encyclical Letter 'Laudato Si' of the Holy Father Francis on Care for Our Common Home," Pt. 2, May 24, 2015.

25. Michael Curry, "Statement in Support of the Advocacy of the People of Standing Rock Sioux Nation," August 25, 2016.

too much. Calling them heretics or pantheists. Firing them from teaching posts.

But faith traditions fully contain the view that God is in nature. You could make a list of names, like a litany of faithful Christians who understood and gave testimony: Thomas Berry, Teilhard de Chardin, Meister Eckhart, Hildegard of Bingen, Paul Tillich, Simone Weil. Then, there are my people, the Celts, who only bowed to full-on, Roman-style Christianity at the very last minute, and even then had quite a few pockets of resistance. The Celts followed the Christianity of Saint John, with his more mystical bent. God, for John, was the Light of Life. (I am indebted to John Philip Newell for much of my information on Celtic Christianity.) The Celts honored their druid ancestors and their monasteries were often placed near or in druidic forest groves.

The Roman mission did not love this point of view. In 664 they met at Whidbey, and the Romans won. On Lindisfarne, where the Celtic mission had worshipped outside, in the wind and fog, a sturdy stone church was built. But the Celtic way did not fully die out and many of its followers became teachers. One of them was a ninth-century man, John Scotus Eriugena, who said that God is the "Life Force" within all things. "Therefore every visible and invisible creature can be called a theophany."[26]

Martin Luther put it beautifully in one of his Table Talks. He tells the story of how his wife, Katie, complained that he was always talking about Christ's presence as being something in the here and now, but she cannot see him. Where is this Lord Christ of whom you constantly speak? she asked. Luther responds that Christ is everywhere, "in the beans in your bean garden, Katie; in the rocks out there, and even in the rope around some poor hopeless man's neck."

---

26. John Scotus Eriugena, *Periphyseon: On the Division of Nature in Celtic Christian Spirituality: Essential Writings*, ed. Mary C. Earle (Woodstock, Vermont: Skylight Paths, 2011), 23.

Christ—this man who died and then was somehow alive again—is present, is everywhere. In the beans in your bean garden, in the waters of the lakes and rivers and mountains, and even in the rope around some poor hopeless man's neck.

And Jesus himself says it in Matthew's Gospel: The kingdom of heaven is in mustard that grows on the hillsides until birds nest in it. The kingdom of God is in yeast a woman "concealed" in bread. The kingdom of God is in what an oyster creates out of a grain of sand.

## The Kingdom Is Here

We have long divided ourselves from the world, thinking of it as the Other, separate from us. Heaven as a place somewhere else, maybe in the sky, beyond. At its worst, this theology divides human beings from where we were born and where we live, and defines us as the part of life that is capable of holiness and the rest . . . not. It also blinds us to the living reality around us, its *ongoingness*, its unfolding. Its solace.

The world is not the Other. It is us. We've grown used to thinking of Matthew's parables as metaphors, and they may well be. But they also may describe Reality. They may describe what is called not pantheism, but panentheism: God in the world, and all in God. The two things, God and world, are not two, but one. They are inseparable.

In the parables, the kingdom of heaven is everywhere, and it's both visible and invisible. The more we know from the work of physicists, the more we know of the visible and the invisible, the wave and the particle. We know that the very material from which life arose was dust blown here from some distant star that we will never see. The world is made of shapes and material that move and change, things we cannot see exactly but often can only apprehend.

**Panentheism:** God is in the world, and all the world is in God.

The woman who put leaven in the bread may have concealed it because she knew it was dangerous and subversive and alive. It was in the bread she baked because it was in her. It's in us, in our skin.

Deep in our Scripture, and deep in our tradition, is this fundamental truth: the kingdom of heaven is right here, under our noses, in things, not separate from them, in the air, in the floors, in the waters, in the rocks, in the beans, and in the daily, heartbreaking reality of our lives—in the sweat, in the blood, and in the tears.

## A Theological, Environmental Crisis

And thus our ministry, our obligation? Last summer, after our first hike, we suffered through days of heat and dry weather in the mountains. Fires burned in Canada to the north, turning the sky a foul gray. I knew what it meant when people prayed for rain. If we understand the full implication of the world as not separable from us, or from God, then we understand what it means to be in what we call an "environmental" crisis. We are in an environmental crisis, but more than that, we are in a theological crisis. We have pushed ourselves so far away from the world that we believe we can treat it as a kind of bottomless candy store, made for our pleasure. On our one and only planet, we are using up the resources of 1½ planets. If sin is separation from God, this is sin.

In the mountains last summer, after three days of smoke and heat, we watched the sky one afternoon as the storm gathered. And when the first huge drops hit the windows, we ran outside. We let the water fall on our faces and I knew what is meant by Blessing. A blessing is a reprieve.

If we imagine the kingdom of heaven as separate from Earth, God is somewhere we can't quite imagine— *out there* certainly a place we have

We have pushed ourselves so far away from the world that we believe we can treat it as a kind of bottomless candy store, made for our pleasure.

never been. And those who die, die *out*, go up *somewhere*. But if we take the parables seriously, if the kingdom of heaven is mustard growing on a hillside in such an abundance of life that it grows (miraculously) into a tree that shields and nurtures the birds of the air. If the kingdom of heaven is like yeast that lifts and ferments and (miraculously) makes flour and water into delicious bread. If the kingdom of heaven is a pearl that forms (miraculously) out of sand . . . then there is another way to think about dying, and where we go. Instead, we die in, that is *reenter* earth, to become part of the world that gave us our beginning, to become part of all that lives, and moves, and has its being. And maybe we, too, become, miraculously, something new.

This is a theology that fits with our tradition, yet heals the divide that has caused us to feel isolated and arrogant. We are part of an ongoing, vital creation as beloved as the lilies of the field and the sparrow that falls to the ground.

God *was* in that hospital emergency room because Anne was there. Because the doctors and nurses were there. Because I was there. The kingdom of heaven was in that room because human beings who are part of the earth were there. And love was there in its final, stubborn, and most heartbreaking form: that we go on loving someone even after he is dead.

This is the story Jesus would have told Anne and me. He did not rescue her or me, because he would not rescue us from grief. He will not rescue us from grief because he will not rescue us from love. This is the visible and invisible essence of all things. This is the Spirit that Michael Curry speaks of as "fully inhabiting Jesus." It's dangerous, subversive, and alive. It offers us, always, a second chance.

## QUESTIONS FOR THE ROAD . . .

**1.** Have you ever encountered God in "the world"?
Where and how has it happened?

**2.** Gallagher says people of faith have divided ourselves from the earth, imagining heaven and God
being some place far away. When have you wit-
nessed this kind of separation? What message or
resource do you find in this chapter that addresses
this divide?

# Chapter 9

# On Leadership for the Movement

## Robert Wright

The Jesus Movement, to my mind, has everything to do with the work of reconciling the human family: upholding the dignity of every human being; actively confronting evil in all its forms; experiencing the abundant life and joy that comes from co-creating with God. It is the people of God enthusiastically living into the promises of our baptism.

While many of us long and pray for a future marked by reconciliation, dignity, and abundant life, just as many lose hope because of what it takes to achieve the dream. Eventually, you have to slog through the inglorious work of holding steady in the face of the resistance, suffering, and loss that inevitably accompany movement. Someone needs to maintain focus so the group can discern what must be carried forward and what must be left behind.

At the very same time, the world is moving at high velocity fueled by high anxiety. We join Jesus's movement even as we may despair over an information and technology revolution that has not revolutionized the ability of the human family to be reconciled.

Martin Luther King Jr.'s reflection holds as true today as when he wrote it in 1956:

> You have allowed your mentality to outrun your morality. You have allowed your civilization to outdistance your culture. Through your scientific genius you have made of the world a neighborhood, but through your moral and spiritual genius you have failed to make of it a brotherhood. So America, I would urge you to keep your moral advances abreast with your scientific advances.[27]

To be faithful to the Jesus Movement and specifically to lead a community following the movement, we will need to knowingly engage the gap King speaks of—the gap between present realities and our stated aspirations as a church and a nation.

For me, that gap is where a concept known as adaptive leadership becomes salient. Ronald Heifetz has written reams on the topic, including *Leadership without Easy Answers* and *Leadership on the Line*, and these texts are field manuals for anyone looking for reliable coordinates to navigate the disorienting map that is modern change leadership. There is a synergy between this type of leadership and the leadership behaviors of Jesus, and it gives me hope for the future of the movement.

## Accept the Adaptive Challenge

The real work of the Jesus Movement is adaptation. It is worth mentioning that the Book of Common Prayer also describes the work of the Church this way. In the preface we read: "Upon weighty and important considerations, according to the various

---

27. Martin Luther King Jr., "Paul's Letter to American Christians," Dexter Avenue Baptist Church, November 4, 1956, https://kinginstitute.stanford.edu/king-papers/.

exigencies of times and occasions, such changes and alterations should be made."[28]

And so, from Jesus, Heifetz, and the Prayer Book, there is a call to make central the work of shifting values, norms, belief

**Adaptive Leadership** is the capacity to mobilize people to address tough problems they'd rather avoid.

systems, and worldviews. We pursue the learning that involves distinguishing what must be conserved from what is expendable. Then we face, sequence, and process the loss that is necessary to refashion old loyalties and develop new competencies. This is the work Jesus is taking on every time he says, "You have heard, but I say to you . . ."

Closer to where I live, in the American South, then governor Nikki Haley of South Carolina took up adaptive work in 2015 after the murder of nine people at Mother Emmanuel African Methodist Episcopal Church. Because the perpetrator was perversely inspired by Confederate history and its flag, Haley led the effort to remove the Confederate flag from the grounds of the South Carolina State House. "This flag, while an integral part of our past, does not represent the future of our great state," she said.[29] As the state's leader, Haley announced they would not shy from the adaptive challenge before them.

For Jesus and his followers, the adaptive work was to announce and embody a kingdom that included a cross, not a king. For Mary his mother, it was living with the uncertainty and sacrificial vulnerability that comes with saying "yes" to God. For Paul, it was the calamity and outlaw status that occurs when you proclaim, "Caesar is not God. Jesus is Lord!"

---

28. BCP, 9.

29. Jeremy Diamond and Dana Bash, "Nikki Haley Calls for Removal of Confederate Flag from Capitol Grounds," June 24, 2015, http://www.cnn.com/2015/06/22/politics/nikki-haley-confederate-flag-south-carolina-press-conference/.

## What Is Your Purpose?

"Power lacking purpose is bankrupt and meaningless."
—Ronald Heifetz[30]

Centrality of purpose is crucial to both Jesus's and Heifetz's leadership activity. Purpose is first and foremost about fire. As science teaches us, the cosmos was born of fire. At the threshold of Moses's new life with God, at the beginning of the church two thousand years ago, it was fire first. When God does something new, there is always fire. For us, purpose is the fire that warms the heart, burns away distractions, gives light for vision, and generates energy to create allies and to sustain the work.

In fact, the root of the word purpose is the Indo-European word "pur" for fire. As in Jesus's introduction of himself in Luke 12, "I came to bring fire. . . ." This fire is different from our work-a-day passions, the things we agree with or "like" and share on Facebook. In a world of competing passions, passion is to purpose as lavender is to purple. Purpose is what is visceral, what is necessary. If vision answers the "where" question, and mission answers the "what" question, then only purpose can answer the "why" question. You might say leadership activity is a consequence of purpose.

Years ago, preaching at our cathedral in Atlanta, Bishop Mdimi Mhogolo of Central Tanganyika asked the clergy of the diocese a thrilling and haunting question: "What is the Diocese of Atlanta believing for?" That's a purpose question. It made everyone pause and imagine our 112 congregations *could* be united in purpose, prayer, and effort toward a preferred future.

---

30. Ronald Heifetz, "The Scholarly/Practical Challenge of Leadership," in *Reflections on Leadership*, ed. Richard Cuoto (Lanham, MD: University Press of America, 2007), 31.

Jesus was raised in a purposeful family. At his conception, his mother was clear that she existed for the purposes of the almighty, "Let it be with me according to your word" (Luke 1:38). From Jesus's preadolescent mouth we hear, "I must be in my Father's house" (Luke 2:49). At the beginning of Jesus's public ministry, he gathers people based on purpose: "I will make you fish for people" (Matt. 4:19). Even in the agony of the Garden of Gethsemane, where Jesus faced betrayal and suffering before his crucifixion, his purpose remained primary: "Not my will but [God's] be done" (Luke 22:42). Jesus lived on purpose, and his followers must follow his pattern if we're to be effective in movement-making.

Purpose moves us toward what's real and immediate; in other words, toward increased authenticity. That authenticity is an inexhaustible energy form. Life and ministry may be filled with tasks, but until those tasks find meaning and coherence in the real and immediate, they will only sap a community's life. Filled with purpose, we feel unstoppable.

New and deeper partnerships also rise from clear purpose. Organizations and individuals with a clear sense of purpose become positively charged magnets bringing people together across silos. In fact, maybe the best feature of purposeful partnerships is the momentum they create for innovation. You only have to watch a jazz band to understand this point. Each virtuoso takes his turn at improvisation, but it always stems from a commonly held tone, tempo, and framework.

Finally, common purpose gives us the ability to talk in terms of results as we move forward. Groups with a clear, shared purpose can invest, measure, learn, and course correct when necessary. So remember, fire first!

## It's Time to Move

"Leadership is the capacity to mobilize people to address
tough problems—especially problems people would
rather avoid." —Ronald Heifetz [31]

Notice, there is no reference to traits, pedigree, role, or "special
sauce" in this definition. What is necessary for leadership is a
commitment to enlarging one's capacity to mobilize people to address the problems that bedevil us as a culture and a world, the
very problems we actively avoid. In this model, "leader" is not
what one is or aspires to be called. Leadership is what you do.
Leadership is activity.

Jesus embodies this model. He is a non-credentialed son of a
day laborer. His followers have no experience at community orga-
nizing and public speaking. However, their leadership paradigm
is clear: aligned in purpose, they mobilize themselves and others,
and with each lesson learned, they increase their capacity. If Jesus
does anything in the three years of his public ministry, he democ-
ratizes the notion of leadership. In Jesus's economy, fisherman can
preach. Samaritans can teach Jewish clergy how to be neighbors.
Those most afraid of Jesus's cross become its chief heralds.

I recently saw a congregation practicing this very notion of
leadership. Faced with rapidly declining attendance and declining revenue, a congregation, call it St. John's, reluctantly released
their full-time minister. Mathematically, the decision was a logical
one and many settled in for the long march toward the inevitable
closing of the church. One distraught layperson came to me determined he would not allow his church to die. He was a man with a
clear purpose. For my part, I assigned the congregation the most
able interim priest available.

---

31. Ronald A. Heifetz, *Leadership without Easy Answers* (Cambridge, MA:
Belknap Harvard, 1994), 15.

What happened in a little more than a year was astounding. In short order the lay-person and minister systematically surfaced several key issues: the inward-facing nature of the congregation and the lack of diversity within the church (even though it was located in a thriving Hispanic neighborhood).

> Organizations and individuals with a clear sense of purpose become positively charged magnets bringing people together across silos.

Together they increased the circle of allies who agreed on the clear purpose of revitalizing the life of the congregation—that is, they claimed a preferred future. Together they increased the sense of shared responsibility for the adaptation that needed to happen if the congregation was going to rise again. Together they faced the feelings of loss. Together, they began to move.

While there are too many details to share here, I can say today this formerly depressed congregation has two new priests, one Anglo and one Hispanic. And the Hispanic congregation is among the fastest growing congregations in the diocese. Instead of cobwebs, you'll see children covering the playground equipment. Pine trees have been removed to construct a soccer field for the community at large.

## Try, Fail, Try Again

"We did the best we could and hoped we'd get another day to try it all over again." —Andrew Young[32]

Perhaps the most life-giving aspect of Jesus's leadership behavior is this: there is no failure, only learning. The leadership activity of Jesus is entirely experimental. You see it in Jesus's sending out of his disciples and Paul's pin-balling missionary endeavors.

---

32. Andrew Young, conversation with author, 2014.

Experimentation is also one of the key elements of adaptive leadership. We run experiments directed toward achieving ends defined by shared purpose. After we experiment, we gather, reflect, refine, and head back out to run a better experiment the next time. This work is highly iterative. It also increases your capacity to live with profound messiness. It is impossible to do adaptive work without experimentation.

I saw this clearly in a conversation with Andrew Young, who was Martin Luther King Jr.'s companion and co-conspirator. Keep in mind, I'm a student of movement leadership people like Jim Lawson, Diane Nash, Marian Wright Edelman, and Young. It was Lawson and Nash who strategized and implemented lunch counter sit-ins that desegregated downtown Nashville. It is Edelman who still builds a movement to defend American children from poverty. It was Young in Montgomery, Alabama, who helped to sustain the movement that broke the back of segregation in public transit.

Ambassador Young reminded me that while history has bundled the story of civil rights into neat, compelling books and documentaries, what is more true is the raw uncertainty, hopeful experiments, crushing disappointments, and sheer providence that resulted in the advance of civil and human rights in America. In short, he said to me, "We did the best we could and hoped we'd get another day to try it all over again."

Thank God he and so many whose names we will never know got up the next day and ran another experiment toward the preferred future of our country, the future so eloquently stated in America's founding documents.

## From Despair to Hope

It is true: fewer people attend church worship services than once did in America, and it is a sign of a dramatic shift in the religious habits of Americans. Yet I am convinced despair is not the best or most faithful response in this liminal moment. The best response is a call to candid questioning and faithful action. This activity will hold in tension the holy trinity of reality, grief, and hope that is the substance of movement work. This faithful action will enflesh the life and longings of Jesus of Nazareth, the stories of faithful people we call the saints, and the wise insights of authors and teachers like Ron Heifetz.

No uber-Christians or outsized leaders will descend from mountaintop experiences to intervene on our behalf. The full answer will not come in the form of the latest book commended by the *New York Times*. We who have the problems, we who follow Jesus in his movement—cocreating with God, we are the people with the fire, the will, and the resilience to solve our most vexing human problems. That is what Jesus taught, and he is with us, even to the end of days (Matt. 28:20).

## QUESTIONS FOR THE ROAD . . .

**1.** Have you ever been part of a group with a clear sense of purpose? How did they achieve it? What were they able to do as a result? What did it feel like to be part of such a group?

**2.** Ronald Heifetz says, "Leadership is the capacity to mobilize people to address tough problems—especially problems people would rather avoid."[33] What problems do you see churches trying to avoid? If you're part of a church or ministry, what do you wish they would finally address and transform? How could you help to lead?

---

33. Heifetz, *Leadership without Easy Answers*, 15.

# Looking Back to Look Forward

## Michael Curry

The Jesus Movement is not a fanciful if inspiring notion for the moment. It is not a quick fix for a long-term problem. It is a solemn call to return, to reclaim the deepest roots of who we are as followers of Jesus Christ, and thereby to reorient ourselves in a time of profound disorientation. Imagine it this way . . .

In 1991 in New York a construction crew was working on a building. They were engaged in some serious unearthing in order to redo the footings and such. They dug and dug and one day they stumbled onto something underground that they never anticipated. It was a small burial ground containing the bodies of Africans in America, some free and some slaves.

The crew hit pause and brought in archaeologists and anthropologists and other experts, because they realized they had stumbled onto sacred ground. One of those experts studied one of the coffins, and found there an insignia, an artistic symbol. It appeared to be a bird moving forward with its head turned backward. Some had no idea what they were seeing, until an anthropologist exclaimed, "That is Sankofa from Ghana, a symbol among the

Ashanti and others. That is an ancient symbol of a very deep and ancient wisdom tradition of West Africa."

Now Sankofa is very often depicted with a chicken; sometimes it's another bird, but the point is that the bird is moving forward, with a clear sense of direction, but it's oriented because it is looking at its past, gleaning wisdom from its heritage, getting strength and courage necessary to go forward with a sense of direction, integrity, and purpose. Sankofa.

I want to suggest that framing our ministry and practice as participation in the Jesus Movement is an exercise in Sankofa. We're doing what Jesus taught us: looking back at the very same time we're looking forward.

Because if you look at the Bible, what you're going to see is the Jesus Movement. If you look at the early Christians, what you're going to see is the Jesus Movement. Now imagine what would happen if people looked at this Episcopal Church, at our ministries of evangelism and reconciliation, with young adults and communities of color, with the earth and with all manner of change . . . imagine if they looked at us and saw Jesus and his movement.

I can see it. I can see us committing heart and mind and soul to following the way of Jesus, the way of God's liberating and life-giving love. And that love really will set us all free.